You Don't Believe It?

Well, you should! Because Ripley's research-ers have done it again! Believe it or not, they have come up with still another collection of unbeatable feats to boggle your brain and frazzle your mind! You still don't believe it? Well, read on . . .

If you cannot find your favorite **Believe It or Not!** POCKET BOOK at your local newsstand, please write to the nearest Ripley's "Believe It or Not!" museum:

19 San Marco Avenue,
St. Augustine, Florida 32084

901 North Ocean Blvd.,
Myrtle Beach, South Carolina 29577

175 Jefferson Street,
San Francisco, California 94133

145 East Elkhorn Avenue,
Estes Park, Colorado 80517

Rebel Corners,
Gatlinburg, Tennessee 37738

1500 North Wells Street,
Chicago, Illinois 60610

4960 Clifton Hill,
Niagara Falls, Canada L2G 3N5

Boardwalk and Wicomico,
Ocean City, Maryland 21842

Ripley's Believe It or Not! titles

Ripley's Believe It or Not! 2nd Series
Ripley's Believe It or Not! 3rd Series
Ripley's Believe It or Not! 4th Series
Ripley's Believe It or Not! 5th Series
Ripley's Believe It or Not! 6th Series
Ripley's Believe It or Not! 7th Series
Ripley's Believe It or Not! 8th Series
Ripley's Believe It or Not! 9th Series
Ripley's Believe It or Not! 10th Series
Ripley's Believe It or Not! 11th Series
Ripley's Believe It or Not! 12th Series
Ripley's Believe It or Not! 13th Series
Ripley's Believe It or Not! 14th Series
Ripley's Believe It or Not! 15th Series
Ripley's Believe It or Not! 16th Series
Ripley's Believe It or Not! 17th Series
Ripley's Believe It or Not! 18th Series
Ripley's Believe It or Not! 19th Series
Ripley's Believe It or Not! 20th Series
Ripley's Believe It or Not! 21st Series
Ripley's Believe It or Not! 22nd Series
Ripley's Believe It or Not! 23rd Series
Ripley's Believe It or Not! 24th Series
Ripley's Believe It or Not! 25th Series
Ripley's Believe It or Not! 26th Series
Ripley's Believe It or Not! 27th Series
Ripley's Believe It or Not! 28th Series
Ripley's Believe It or Not! 29th Series
Ripley's Believe It or Not! 30th Series
Ripley's Believe It or Not! Anniversary Edition
Ripley's Believe It or Not! Book of Americana
Ripley's Believe It or Not! Book of the Military
Ripley's Believe It or Not! Book of Undersea Oddities
Ripley's Believe It or Not! Ghosts, Witches, and ESP
Ripley's Believe It or Not! Stars, Space, and UFOs
Ripley's Believe It or Not! Tombstones and Graveyards

Published by POCKET BOOKS

Ripley's
Believe It or Not!®

30th SERIES

PUBLISHED BY POCKET BOOKS NEW YORK

Another *Original* publication of POCKET BOOKS

 POCKET BOOKS, a Simon & Schuster division of
GULF & WESTERN CORPORATION
1230 Avenue of the Americas, New York, N.Y. 10020

ISBN: 0-671-82067-2

First Pocket Books printing May, 1979

10 9 8 7 6 5 4 3 2 1

Trademarks registered in the United States and other countries.

Printed in the U.S.A.

PREFACE

The number thirty is many things to many people, especially symbolizing the coming of age. But, to us here at Ripley's, it takes a very special significance represented by this book you have in hand. In celebration of this thirtieth Ripley's edition, we have searched our archives to cull those fascinating oddities that pertain to the number thirty.

Consider this, just for starters: On the thirtieth of September, 1846, ether was used during the extraction of a tooth for the first time!

On the thirtieth of January, 1897, the sale of intoxicating drinks to Indians was prohibited by law.

Other notable historical events involving the number thirty include—

The death of Cleopatra, Queen of Egypt. On August 30, 30 B.C., she killed herself by clasping an asp to her bosom.

The purchase of Alaska, on March 30, 1867. (We bought it from the Russians for $7,200,000—the green stamps alone made it worthwhile!)

The inauguration of George Washington as the first President of the United States, on the thirtieth of April, 1789.

The mysterious disappearance of Supreme Court Justice Joseph F. Crater, on August 6, 1930.

And in December of that same fateful year, the failure of The Bank of the United States, with sixty-two offices in New York City and almost 400,000 depositors.

If it's birthdays you want, thirty is loaded. On the thirtieth of November, 1835, America's greatest humorist, Mark Twain, was born in Monroe County, Florida.

On that same day in 1874, one of England's greatest statesmen was born—Winston Churchill.

November 13th, in 1830, marked the birth of the writer who gave us Dr. Jekyll, Mr. Hyde, and Long John Silver—Robert Louis Stevenson.

And if cities can have a birthday, New York had its own on the fifteenth of January, 1730, the day it was granted a royal charter.

But why, you may ask, all this hoopla about the number thirty?

Like its many illustrious predecessors, this thirtieth edition is packed with the fascinating people, places and things that have made the name "Ripley's" synonymous with "incredible" for exactly half a century now!

See for yourself—just look inside!

Ripley International Limited
Toronto, Canada

Ripley's Believe It or Not!

THE MOST AMAZING ALPINIST IN ALL HISTORY! SIR FRANCIS JOSEPH CAMPBELL (1832-1914) CLIMBED MONT BLANC (15,771')-- HIGHEST PEAK IN THE ALPS-- ALTHOUGH HE HAD BEEN BLIND FROM THE AGE OF 4 (1880)

IVAN HOLM A STOCKBROKER OF ST. PETERSBURG, RUSSIA, ATTENDED 600 BALLET PERFORMANCES ANNUALLY FOR A PERIOD OF 50 YEARS --A TOTAL OF 30,000 PERFORMANCES INCLUDING REHEARSALS

CHICKEN THAT LAYS *ONLY GREEN EGGS* Submitted by MRS. JOYCE MATTEI New Orleans, La.

THE **MEMORIAL** TO THE **YOUNGEST** "OLD MAN!" Amritsar, India,

THE TOWER OF BABA ATAL *THE NAME OF WHICH MEANS OLD MAN ATAL* HAS ONE FLOOR FOR EACH YEAR OF ATAL RAI'S AGE AT HIS DEATH IN 1628 - AT THE AGE OF 9! *HE WAS REVERED AS OLD MAN ATAL BECAUSE OF HIS WISDOM AND LEARNING*

10

THE CHILD WHO CROSSED THE ALPS ON FOOT !
FREGGE von HALLBERG-BROICH (1818-1845)
WALKED FROM MUNICH, GERMANY, TO ROME, ITALY,
A DISTANCE OF **500** MILES
WHEN SHE WAS ONLY 8 YEARS OF AGE
(1826)

A **BOARD**
3/4 OF AN INCH THICK
THAT BECAME **6** INCHES
THICK IN A PERIOD OF
13 YEARS BY ADDITION
*OF 5,000 COATS
OF PAINT*
Submitted by
PETE PETERSON
Washington, D.C.

Emperor **LEOPOLD I**
(1640-1705) of Germany
AWARE THAT HE WAS DYING,
SUMMONED THE IMPERIAL ORCHESTRA
TO HIS BEDCHAMBER SO THAT
*HIS LAST RECOLLECTION WOULD
BE BEAUTIFUL MUSIC*

THE **LONGKIBUTS**
DIG UP THEIR DEAD
AFTER 3 MONTHS AND
*INTER THE BODY IN
A SEATED POSITION IN
A NICHE CUT INTO A
WOOD COLUMN, ERECTED
BEHIND THE HUT IN
WHICH HE LIVED*
(Borneo)

AN ANCIENT ROMAN COIN
THAT CARRIED THE
OUTLINE OF AN OX
*BECAUSE IT WAS JUST THE
PRICE OF THAT ANIMAL*

THE **MAN** WHO WAS NEVER LATE!
ALDERMAN WILLIAM NEILD
(1789-1864) of Manchester, England,
WAS SO PUNCTUAL THAT HIS FELLOW
CITIZENS SET THEIR WATCHES BY
HIS COMINGS AND GOINGS

*HE AROSE SUDDENLY AT A
COMMITTEE MEETING IN TOWN HALL,
PULLED OUT HIS WATCH, ANNOUNCED,
"TIME IS UP, GENTLEMEN!"
-AND DROPPED DEAD*

THE **CHANTING GOSHAWK**
OF SOUTH AFRICA
IS THE ONLY BIRD
OF PREY *THAT SINGS*

THE **LEANING TOWER**
OF LA VERMONDIE
in France
TILTS 3 FEET

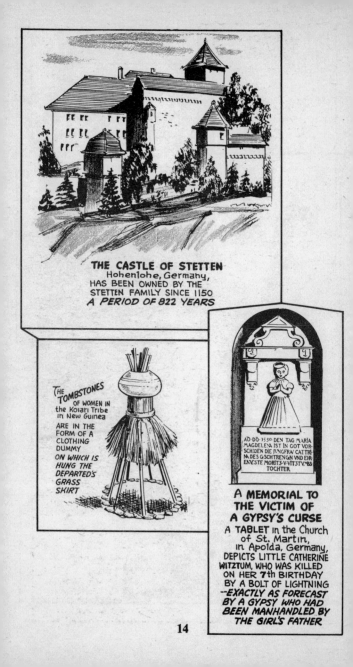

THE CASTLE OF STETTEN
Hohenlohe, Germany,
HAS BEEN OWNED BY THE
STETTEN FAMILY SINCE 1150
A PERIOD OF 822 YEARS

THE **TOMBSTONES**
OF WOMEN in
the Koiari Tribe
in New Guinea
ARE IN THE
FORM OF A
CLOTHING
DUMMY
*ON WHICH IS
HUNG THE
DEPARTED'S
GRASS
SKIRT*

AD·DO·1550·DEN TAG MARIA
MAGDELENA IST IN GOT VORSCHIDEN DIE IVNGFRAV CATTRINA DES GSCHTRENGN VND EHRENVESTE MORITS·V·VITSTV·BS
TOCHTER

**A MEMORIAL TO
THE VICTIM OF
A GYPSY'S CURSE**
A TABLET in the Church
of St. Martin,
in Apolda, Germany,
DEPICTS LITTLE CATHERINE
WITZTUM, WHO WAS KILLED
ON HER **7**th BIRTHDAY
BY A BOLT OF LIGHTNING
*--EXACTLY AS FORECAST
BY A GYPSY WHO HAD
BEEN MANHANDLED BY
THE GIRL'S FATHER*

THE **COAT OF ARMS** of Sauve, France, FEATURES A BRANCH OF SAGE AND THE WORDS, SAL SAL --*LATIN FOR* "*SAVED BY SAGE*"-- BECAUSE CENTURIES AGO WHEN AN EPIDEMIC RAVAGED THE TOWN *RESIDENTS WERE SAVED BY EATING SAGE*

THE **FIRST WRITING INSTRUMENT** *A BONE STYLUS* USED IN CUNEIFORM WRITING *4,000 YEARS AGO*

THE **MONARCH** WHO HEARD WITH HIS MOUTH! SULTAN SOLIMAN (1646-1694) of Persia BECAUSE OF A MALFORMATION OF HIS AUDITORY CANALS COULD HEAR ONLY BY *OPENING HIS MOUTH*

THE **EASTER CHURCH**
Saalfelden, Austria

A **CHAPEL** CONSTRUCTED IN A CAVE IN A MOUNTAIN HAS HELD ONLY ONE SERVICE EACH YEAR --ON EASTER SUNDAY-- *FOR NEARLY 300 YEARS*

THE CHAPEL SERVES THE REST OF THE YEAR AS A LOOKOUT POST FOR A FIRE GUARD WHO SOUNDS THE ALARM WHEN A BLAZE IS SPOTTED IN THE COMMUNITY BELOW HIM

THE **AFRICAN FERRARIA** WITHERS AND DIES AFTER BLOOMING FOR *ONLY HALF A DAY*

THE **MAN WHO COULDN'T BE KILLED!**
JACQUES de la FORCE
(1558-1652)

A POLITICAL FOE OF SIX FRENCH KINGS, SURVIVED WITHOUT A SCRATCH ALTHOUGH HE WAS

"EXECUTED" BY A FIRING SQUAD AT THE AGE OF 14 AND CONDEMNED TO DEATH BY THREE MONARCHS

HE SURVIVED TO BECOME A DUKE AND FIELD MARSHAL OF FRANCE AND DIED IN BED AT THE AGE OF 94

THE MAN WHO NEVER CLOSED HIS EYES!

THEODORE CORNETTE (1835-1890) of Paris, France, A NOTORIOUS MISER: WHO KEPT $250,000 IN GOLD AND CURRENCY HIDDEN IN HIS HOME AFTER A DOZEN ROBBERIES, *LEARNED TO SLEEP WITH HIS EYES OPEN* FOR **23** YEARS HE NEVER CLOSED HIS EYES--AND WAS NOT ROBBED DURING THAT ENTIRE PERIOD

FOX TRAPS CONSTRUCTED BY THE ESKIMOS OF GREENLAND, CONSIST OF ROCKS BALANCED ONE ATOP ANOTHER SO THAT WHEN THE ANIMAL REACHES FOR A PIECE OF MEAT *A HEAVY STONE WILL FALL ON HIM*

THE **LEAP YEAR** FAMILY
JOSEPH ETTA (1816-1890) of Paris, France, AND HIS SON, ARMAND, LIVED A TOTAL OF **144 YEARS** --YET CELEBRATED ONLY **35 BIRTHDAYS** THE FATHER WAS BORN ON **FEB. 29, 1816** AND THE SON ON **FEB. 29,** 1840

18

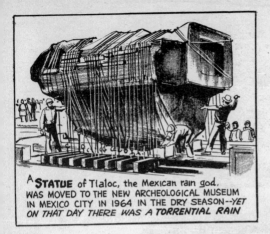

A **STATUE** of Tlaloc, the Mexican rain god,
WAS MOVED TO THE NEW ARCHEOLOGICAL MUSEUM
IN MEXICO CITY IN 1964 IN THE DRY SEASON--YET
ON THAT DAY THERE WAS A TORRENTIAL RAIN

THE
SKULL
of
ST. YVES
(1253 -1303)
PATRON SAINT
OF FRENCH
ATTORNEYS
*IS DISPLAYED
IN THE CATHEDRAL
OF TREGUIER*

THE CHAPEL OF SAINT-LAMBERT
in Le Hoyoux, Belgium,
IS VISITED BY TOOTHACHE SUFFERERS
WHO BELIEVE THEY CAN ACHIEVE RELIEF
BY BITING ITS STONE WALL

THE CRUELEST HUSBAND IN ALL HISTORY!
SULTAN IBRAHIM (1615-1648) OF TURKEY
BORED BY HIS ENTIRE HAREM
HAD HIS 1,000 WIVES AND CONCUBINES SEWN INTO INDIVIDUAL SACKS AND DROWNED THEM IN THE BOSPHORUS!

AL SHEAN
BORN MAY 12, 1868
I COULD HAVE
LIVED LONGER
BUT NOW IT'S TOO LATE.
ABSOLUTELY, MR. GALLAGHER
--POSITIVELY, MR. SHEAN
AUG. 12, 1949

Epitaph OF THE VAUDEVILLE ENTERTAINER IN MT. PLEASANT CEMETERY, PLEASANTVILLE, NEW YORK

CALL ME SUGAR!

TWO EGG, a town in Florida, WAS NAMED FOR A SYSTEM OF BARTER USED IN THE AREA AFTER THE CIVIL WAR, *WHEN TWO EGGS WERE REGULARLY TRADED FOR A BAG OF TOBACCO OR SUGAR*

CIRCULAR CHESSBOARD COTTONIAN LIBRARY OF THE BRITISH MUSEUM, LONDON

THE **STRANGEST SIGNATURE IN HISTORY**

میر محمود

KING MIR MAHMUD (1700-1725) of Persia BECAUSE HE ASCENDED THE THRONE AT THE AGE OF 22 *SIGNED EVERY LETTER AND STATE DOCUMENT 22 TIMES*

21

ANATOLE FRANCE (1844-1924)
1921 WINNER OF THE NOBEL PRIZE FOR LITERATURE, HAD A BRAIN THAT WEIGHED *9½ OUNCES LESS THAN NORMAL*

THE **MAN WHO FEARED HIS OWN POWER!**
JOSEPH FRIEDRICH (1790-1873)
A WOODCARVER OF BERLIN, GERMANY, MADE AN IVORY MINIATURE OF THE CHURCH OF ST. NICHOLAS IN POTSDAM -- *WHICH AFTER A SHORT TIME, DEVELOPED A CRACK.*
A FEW WEEKS LATER THE CHURCH ITSELF DEVELOPED A SIMILAR CRACK IN THE SAME SPOT *-- AND FRIEDRICH DIED OF FRIGHT*

SIMON ARGEVITCH OF OAKLAND, CALIF., CAN WHISTLE WHILE *SIMULTANEOUSLY SMOKING 12 CIGARS*

23

THE GREAT GRANARY CASTLE
OF ID AISSA
IN SOUTHERN MOROCCO
PROVIDING INDIVIDUAL STORAGE
AREAS FOR EACH FARMER'S GRAIN
WAS BUILT BY PILING STONES ONE
ON TOP OF ANOTHER WITHOUT
THE USE OF MORTAR-- YET
IT HAS ENDURED FOR CENTURIES

AN OUTDOOR BATH in Iceland
CONSTRUCTED WITH BLOCKS OF HEWN
STONE IN THE 13th CENTURY AND FED
BY AN UNDERGROUND WARM SPRING
IS STILL INTACT AFTER 700 YEARS

THE **STONE ELEPHANT**
Zanzibar
NATURAL ROCK FORMATION

THAI DANCERS
WEAR AS HEADGEAR
A BASKET AND FLOWERS

THE BELFRY
of the Church of Herisson, France,
LEFT STANDING AFTER THE REST OF
THE EDIFICE WAS DEMOLISHED
NOW HAS A STREET RUNNING THROUGH IT

THE **SPUR-WINGED PLOVER**
OF AFRICA
REPEATEDLY ASKS,
"DID YOU DO IT?"

HENRY CLAY HANSBROUGH
(1848 - 1897)
A U.S. REPRESENTATIVE
FROM ILLINOIS,
LOST HIS BID FOR
RENOMINATION IN 1890,
*BUT STILL SERVED IN
CONGRESS FOR
ANOTHER 6 YEARS BY
SUCCESSFULLY RUNNING
FOR THE U.S. SENATE*

THE BENGLOG FALLS
IN Wales ARE FED BY 2
DIFFERENT STREAMS--ONE
FLOWING FROM LAKE OGWEN
AND THE OTHER FROM LAKE IDWAL
-- *WHICH CROSS EACH OTHER
AT THE TOP OF THE FALLS*

A **CROSS**
CARVED IN A STABLE WALL
in Kleinmachnow, Germany,
AS A MEMORIAL TO A
MAN WHO WAS STABBED
TO DEATH NEARBY--
*BECAUSE, ALTHOUGH
THE KILLER WAS
KNOWN, HE WAS
NEVER PUNISHED*

LORD WEMYSS
(1818 – 1914)
WAS A MEMBER OF THE
CARLTON CLUB IN
LONDON, ENGLAND
FOR 74 YEARS

A **CANDLESTICK**
IN THE
TOWN HALL OF
BREMGARTEN,
SWITZERLAND, IS
FASHIONED IN
THE LIKENESS
OF A
*CHARWOMAN
WHO
WORKED
THERE
FOR YEARS*

A **PEAR TREE** in Danvers, Mass.,
PLANTED BY JOHN ENDICOTT IN 1630,
STILL BEARS FRUIT **348 YEARS LATER**

THE MEMORIAL
TO THE FRENCH WRITER FENELON
(1651-1715) IN CAMBRAI, FRANCE,
ORIGINALLY WAS THE ORNATE
GATE OF THE PALACE
OF THE ARCHBISHOPS

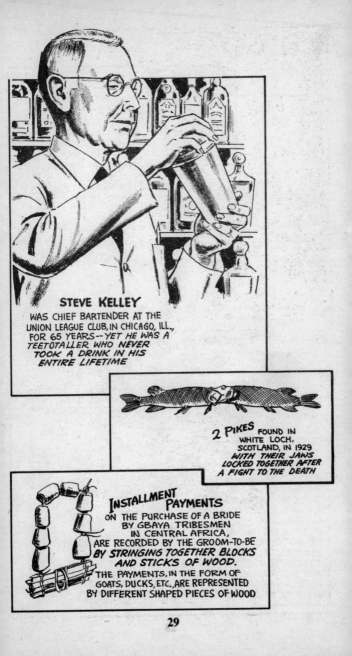

STEVE KELLEY
WAS CHIEF BARTENDER AT THE
UNION LEAGUE CLUB, IN CHICAGO, ILL.,
FOR 65 YEARS-- YET HE WAS A
TEETOTALLER WHO NEVER
TOOK A DRINK IN HIS
ENTIRE LIFETIME

2 PIKES FOUND IN
WHITE LOCH,
SCOTLAND, IN 1929
WITH THEIR JAWS
LOCKED TOGETHER AFTER
A FIGHT TO THE DEATH

INSTALLMENT PAYMENTS
ON THE PURCHASE OF A BRIDE
BY GBAYA TRIBESMEN
IN CENTRAL AFRICA,
ARE RECORDED BY THE GROOM-TO-BE
*BY STRINGING TOGETHER BLOCKS
AND STICKS OF WOOD.*
THE PAYMENTS, IN THE FORM OF
GOATS, DUCKS, ETC., ARE REPRESENTED
BY DIFFERENT SHAPED PIECES OF WOOD

"DICHOSO, NO PIENSA"

THE **SKULL** of VICENTE MARIA VELAZQUEZ, PRIEST OF THE CHURCH OF SAN JUAN BAUTISTA, DISPLAYED IN THE MUSEUM OF MERIDA, MEXICO, BEARS IN SPANISH A LINE WRITTEN ON IT BY POET LUIS ROSADO --"*HE IS LUCKY, HE DOESN'T THINK*"

THE ALPINIST WHOSE STRENGTH SAVED 5 MEN FROM DEATH!
PETER SCHOENING of Seattle, Wash., 26-YEAR-OLD MEMBER OF AN AMERICAN EXPEDITION CLIMBING K-2, A 28,258-FOOT PEAK IN THE HIMALAYAS, ROPED TO 5 COMPANIONS IN A BLINDING SNOWSTORM, *SINGLEHANDEDLY SUPPORTED THE WEIGHT OF ALL 5 MEN WHEN THEY SLIPPED OFF A LEDGE AT A HEIGHT OF 24,000 FEET!* (Aug., 1953)

THE **CHURCH OF CAPRINO VERONESE**
Italy, HAS A DECORATIVE FAÇADE,
BUT ITS SANCTUARY
IS A HUGE CAVE

A **PINE TREE**
in Kyoto, Japan,
*SHAPED LIKE
A SHIP*

THE **LUGWORM**, TO GET THE TINY
ORGANISMS WHICH ARE ITS FOOD,
EATS MUD AND SAND

THE CATHEDRAL IN RIKITEA ON THE ISLAND OF MANGAREVA, THE LARGEST CATHOLIC CATHEDRAL IN THE SOUTH SEAS, CONSTRUCTED TO ACCOMMODATE 2,000 PARISHIONERS IN 1834, TODAY DOES NOT HAVE A SINGLE WORSHIPER

DISCUS FISH ARE NURSED BY THEIR PARENTS

THE VEILED WOMEN OF THE HARASI TRIBE OF HADHRAMAUT, ARABIA, MAY WEAR BLACK MASKS ONLY IF THEIR REPUTATIONS ARE SPOTLESS

THE MOST BIZARRE SMUGGLING OPERATION IN HISTORY!

CALIMENA SAMPUNIA, AN EGYPTIAN ACTRESS APPEARING IN A PLAY IN MARSEILLES, FRANCE, IN 1934, WAS MARRIED TO HER LEADING MAN, CHRIS GOTTAKIS, BUT SUDDENLY COLLAPSED DURING THE CEREMONY· *AND WAS PRONOUNCED DEAD*·

THOUSANDS OF FRENCH PEOPLE CONTRIBUTED TO A WIDELY PUBLICIZED FUND TO SEND HER BODY HOME, BUT POLICE WHO RAIDED THE HOUSE TO WHICH THE COFFIN WAS DELIVERED FOUND IT CONTAINED A WAX REPLICA OF THE BRIDE--WHO WAS VERY MUCH ALIVE-- *AND A SHIPMENT OF HEROIN·*

THE **LANGLEIKE** AN ANCIENT NORWEGIAN STRINGED INSTRUMENT, IS PLAYED BY ANDREAS HAUGE, *THE ONLY MAN IN THE WORLD WHO DOES*

JOHN MYTTON (1796-1834) of Halston, England, CURED HIMSELF OF HICCOUGHING **BY SETTING FIRE TO HIS NIGHTSHIRT!** *HE HAD A NARROW ESCAPE FROM DEATH - BUT IT CURED HIS HICCOUGHS*

THE **BELFRY** of the CATHEDRAL OF ST. THEODORIT in Uzès, France, *IS THE ONLY ROUND CHURCH TOWER IN ALL FRANCE*

A **SHIELD** used by English soldiers in the 16th century WAS EQUIPPED WITH A **BREECH-LOADING PISTOL**

THOSE WHO CARED FOR HIM WHILE LIVING

WILL KNOW WHOSE BODY LIES RESTING HERE, TO OTHERS IT DOES NOT MATTER

Epitaph in Old North Cemetery, Hartford, Conn.

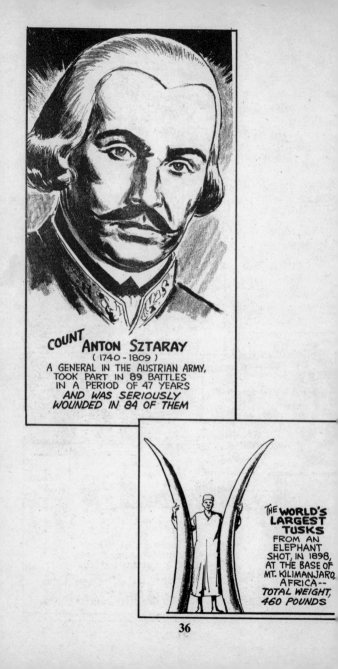

COUNT **Anton Sztaray**
(1740 - 1809)
A GENERAL IN THE AUSTRIAN ARMY,
TOOK PART IN 89 BATTLES
IN A PERIOD OF 47 YEARS
*AND WAS SERIOUSLY
WOUNDED IN 84 OF THEM*

THE **WORLD'S
LARGEST
TUSKS**
FROM AN
ELEPHANT
SHOT, IN 1898,
AT THE BASE OF
MT. KILIMANJARO,
AFRICA --
*TOTAL WEIGHT,
460 POUNDS*

THE COLOR OF THE TURACOU RUNS WHEN IT RAINS

THE SAHATKULA CLOCK TOWER IN SKOPLJE, YUGOSLAVIA, HAS BEEN IN WORKING USE FOR 1,644 YEARS

THE TOMB OF JEHANARA, DAUGHTER OF THE BUILDER OF THE TAJ MAHAL, BEARS AN INSCRIPTION ASKING THAT THE GRASS BE KEPT GREEN ON HER GRAVE

A **CHILD**
BORN IN THE TSIMEHETA TRIBE OF MADAGASCAR
ON A TUESDAY WAS OFTEN SLAIN,
*IN THE BELIEF THAT A TUESDAY INFANT WOULD
BRING ITS PARENTS BAD LUCK*

A **DRINKING HORN**
PRESERVED IN THE CATHEDRAL OF YORK,
ENGLAND, WAS USED IN THE TIME OF
KING CANUTE BY ITS OWNER, ULPHAS, TO
REPRESENT HIS EXTENSIVE ESTATES IN YORKSHIRE
-- WHICH HE PRESENTED TO THE CHURCH

DR. **PHILIP SYNG PHYSICK**
(1768-1837)
KNOWN AS THE FATHER OF AMERICAN SURGERY, SUFFERED AN ATTACK OF YELLOW FEVER IN 1798 AND *WAS BLED OF 11 PINTS OF BLOOD --5½ QUARTS!* AMAZINGLY, HE SURVIVED FOR ANOTHER 38 YEARS

EPITAPH OF HERMON FIFE, A BACHELOR IN NORTH PEMBROKE, N.H. *HE DID NOT INVENT THE REVOLVER*

HERE LIES THE MAN NEVER BEAT BY A PLAN STRAIGHT WAS HIS AIM AND SURE OF HIS GAME NEVER WAS A LOVER BUT INVENTED THE REVOLVER

THE **OLDEST PICTURE OF A WHEEL** FOUND IN THE COURT OF FELINES IN UR, BABYLONIA, AND DRAWN 5,500 YEARS AGO

THE GOLDEN GUN OF THE GAEKWAR
THE CEREMONIAL CANNON
OF THE GAEKWAR, OR RULER, OF BARODA, INDIA,
WEIGHED 280 POUNDS, AND EVEN ITS RAMRODS
WERE SOLID GOLD

THE **LARVA** OF THE
COMMON BLUE
BUTTERFLY,
EXUDES DROPS OF
HONEY THAT ATTRACT
ANTS -- *WHICH
PROTECT THE LARVA
FROM PREDATORS*

THE **3 TOWERS of LUXEMBOURG**
BUILT IN 1050 AS PART OF THE
CITY WALL, SERVED FOR YEARS
AS A HIGH SECURITY PRISON.
THE TOWERS HAD NO ENTRANCES
OR STAIRWAYS AND PRISONERS
AND THEIR FOOD WERE LIFTED
TO THE CELLS BY ROPES

THE **RED-BACKED SHRIKE**
LAYS EGGS WITH SUCH DISTINC-
TIVE MARKINGS, THAT THOSE OF
NO 2 HENS ARE ALIKE

THE AMAZING PILOT PORPOISE OF HATTERAS INLET

"HATTERAS JACK" a white porpoise FOR A PERIOD OF 20 YEARS GUIDED EVERY SHIP IN AND OUT OF HATTERAS INLET, OFF THE COAST OF NORTH CAROLINA-- AND *NEVER LOST A SINGLE VESSEL!*

IT WOULD SWIM AROUND EACH SHIP TO GAUGE ITS SIZE AND DRAW, WAIT UNTIL THE TIDE HAD REACHED THE PROPER LEVEL, THEN LEAD THE VESSEL SAFELY PAST THE TREACHEROUS SHOALS AND REEFS--

"HATTERAS JACK" FIRST APPEARED IN 1790 AND DISAPPEARED IN 1810 WHEN THE PLACING OF BUOYS AND BELLS MADE HIS ASSISTANCE UNNECESSARY

A **CARVING** ON THE CITY HALL OF BRUSSELS, BELGIUM, DEPICTS A JUDGE NAMED HERKENBALD EXECUTING A SENTENCE OF DEATH ON HIS OWN NEPHEW, *BY STRANGLING HIM WITH HIS HANDS*

THE LONGNOSE GAR MUST BREATHE FRESH AIR--*FROM TIME TO TIME STICKING ITS ELONGATED SNOUT ABOVE THE WATER*

THE **SHELL** OF A TRITON'S TRUMPET IS BLOWN THROUGH BY SHINTO PRIESTS IN JAPAN *TO CALL THE FAITHFUL TO WORSHIP*

THE **GOLDEN MADONNA** IN THE CATHEDRAL OF ESSEN, GERMANY, *IS THE OLDEST SCULPTURE OF THE MADONNA*

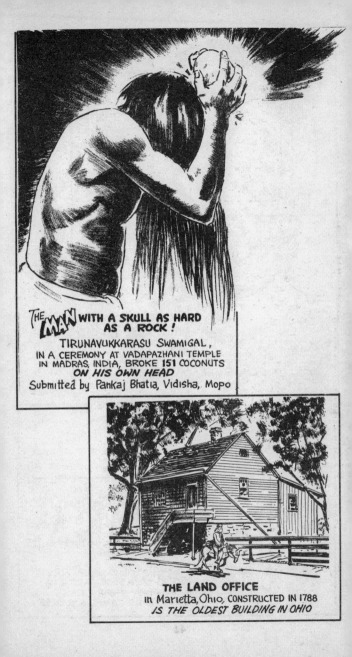

THE **MAN** WITH A SKULL AS HARD AS A ROCK!

TIRUNAVUKKARASU SWAMIGAL, IN A CEREMONY AT VADAPAZHANI TEMPLE IN MADRAS, INDIA, BROKE 151 COCONUTS *ON HIS OWN HEAD*

Submitted by Pankaj Bhatia, Vidisha, Mopo

THE LAND OFFICE
in Marietta, Ohio, CONSTRUCTED IN 1788 *IS THE OLDEST BUILDING IN OHIO*

A MEKEO TRIBESMAN OF NEW GUINEA

WEARS A TURTLE SHELL DISK ON HIS FOREHEAD ONLY IF HE --OR AN ANCESTOR-- HAS KILLED AN ENEMY IN BATTLE

HUTS of the Somali tribesmen of Africa ARE MOVED TO EACH NEW CAMPSITE, AND ON THE JOURNEY THEIR GRASS MAT WALLS SERVE AS CAMEL SADDLES

MOUNT ARARAT
THE PEAK ON WHICH NOAH'S ARK CAME TO REST AFTER THE FLOOD, NOW MARKS THE BORDER OF THE SOVIET UNION, IRAN AND TURKEY

The **MAN WHO KILLED A LION WITH HIS BARE FEET!**

Simba A NATIVE HUNTER OF TANGANYIKA, AFRICA, TREED BY A HUGE LION WHICH HE HAD WOUNDED WITH HIS SPEAR, SAVED HIMSELF AND A COMPANION FROM CERTAIN DEATH BY LEAPING ONTO THE ANIMAL'S BACK FROM A HEIGHT OF 20 FEET. *HIS BARE FEET BROKE THE LION'S BACK*

45

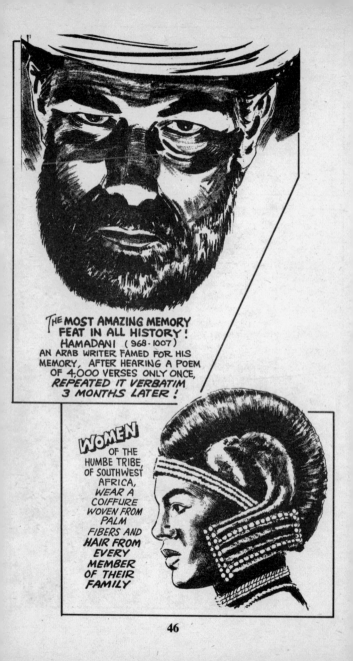

THE MOST AMAZING MEMORY
FEAT IN ALL HISTORY!
HAMADANI (968-1007)
AN ARAB WRITER FAMED FOR HIS
MEMORY, AFTER HEARING A POEM
OF 4,000 VERSES ONLY ONCE,
*REPEATED IT VERBATIM
3 MONTHS LATER!*

WOMEN OF THE
HUMBE TRIBE,
OF SOUTHWEST
AFRICA,
*WEAR A
COIFFURE
WOVEN FROM
PALM
FIBERS AND
HAIR FROM
EVERY
MEMBER
OF THEIR
FAMILY*

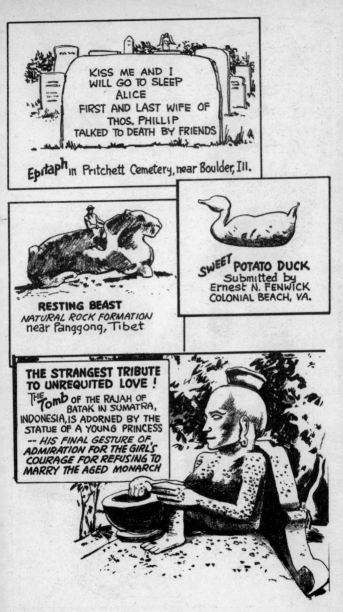

KISS ME AND I
WILL GO TO SLEEP
ALICE
FIRST AND LAST WIFE OF
THOS. PHILLIP
TALKED TO DEATH BY FRIENDS

Epitaph in Pritchett Cemetery, near Boulder, Ill.

RESTING BEAST
NATURAL ROCK FORMATION
near Panggong, Tibet

SWEET POTATO DUCK
Submitted by
Ernest N. FENWICK
COLONIAL BEACH, VA.

**THE STRANGEST TRIBUTE
TO UNREQUITED LOVE!**
The Tomb OF THE RAJAH OF
BATAK IN SUMATRA, IS ADORNED BY THE
INDONESIA, IS ADORNED BY THE
STATUE OF A YOUNG PRINCESS
-- HIS FINAL GESTURE OF
ADMIRATION FOR THE GIRL'S
COURAGE FOR REFUSING TO
MARRY THE AGED MONARCH

THE REV. PHILIP FRAZIER SERVES THE STANDING-ROCK RESERVATION OF NORTH AND SOUTH DAKOTA AS MINISTER OF **5 CHURCHES**

THE DICHEA ORCHID of Brazil HAS A HUMAN FACE

THE GOLD-ENCRUSTED THRONES of the Chiefs of Monana, in the Congo, MUST EACH BE CARVED FROM A **SINGLE BLOCK OF WOOD**

THE **FACADE** of the Monastery of San Bruno, Italy, IS STILL STANDING **872** YEARS AFTER ITS CONSTRUCTION, ALTHOUGH AN EARTHQUAKE, IN 1783, WRECKED THE STRUCTURE, WHIRLED ITS FACADE ENTIRELY AROUND — AND THEN **TURNED IT BACK TO ITS ORIGINAL POSITION!**

THE **LULLABY THAT WAS INSPIRED BY A CALAMITY!**
A YOUNG MUSICIAN in Bonn, Germany,
HAVING VOLUNTEERED TO CARE FOR THE 3-YEAR-OLD SON OF A
LADY BALLOONIST, TOOK THE CHILD TO HIS HOME WHEN THE BALLOON
CRASHED IN FLAMES, AND CALMED THE YOUNGSTER BY COMPOSING A LULLABY
*THE MUSICIAN WAS JOHANNES BRAHMS AND THE PIECE HE COMPOSED
WAS "THE CRADLE SONG"-THE MOST FAMOUS LULLABY IN MUSICAL HISTORY*
-1865

BILLY PEIRSE
(1764-1839)
an English jockey,
READ ONLY 2
BOOKS IN HIS
ENTIRE LIFETIME
–THE BIBLE AND ADAM
SMITH'S "WEALTH OF
NATIONS"–YET HE
READ BOTH OF THOSE
FROM COVER TO COVER
30 TIMES

EACH OF **6** TEAMS IN THE NATIONAL
HOCKEY LEAGUE PLAYED TIE-SCORE
GAMES ON NOV.20,1955-- *AND
EACH TEAM SCORED ONE GOAL*

THE
**CATHEDRAL
OF VERONA**
ITALY,
WAS UNDER
CONSTRUCTION
FOR MORE
THAN **400**
YEARS

THE MOTHER WHO HAD
14 CHILDREN IN 2 YEARS!
BRIGITTE STINGLHEIM
(1365-1410) OF HOHENWART
BEI BURGHAUSEN, GERMANY,
GAVE BIRTH TO SEPTUPLETS
IN 2 SUCCESSIVE YEARS
(1390 -1391)

THE **ALDEN HOUSE** at Duxbury, Mass., IS THE ONLY SURVIVING
STRUCTURE EVER OCCUPIED BY ONE OF THE
PILGRIMS WHO CAME TO AMERICA ON THE MAYFLOWER.
JOHN AND PRISCILLA ALDEN LIVED -
AND DIED- IN THE HOUSE

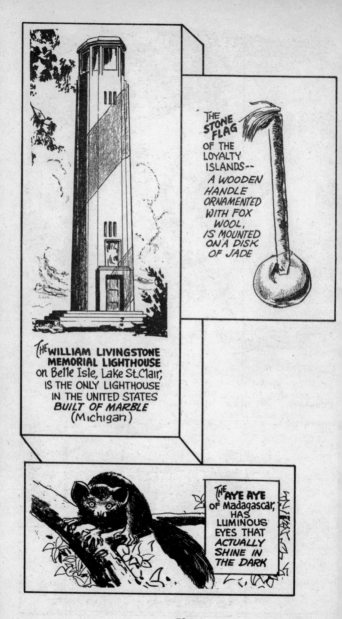

THE **WILLIAM LIVINGSTONE MEMORIAL LIGHTHOUSE** on Belle Isle, Lake St.Clair, IS THE ONLY LIGHTHOUSE IN THE UNITED STATES *BUILT OF MARBLE* (Michigan)

THE **STONE FLAG** OF THE LOYALTY ISLANDS-- *A WOODEN HANDLE ORNAMENTED WITH FOX WOOL, IS MOUNTED ON A DISK OF JADE*

THE **AYE AYE** of Madagascar, HAS LUMINOUS EYES THAT *ACTUALLY SHINE IN THE DARK*

EMPEROR AURELIAN WHO RULED THE ROMAN WORLD FROM 270 TO 275 -- AS A SOLDIER BEFORE HE BECAME RULER, *KILLED 950 ENEMIES IN HAND-TO-HAND COMBAT* ... HE SLEW 48 SARMATIANS IN A SINGLE DAY'S BATTLE

THE INSEL HOTEL in Constance, Germany, ORIGINALLY WAS A DOMINICAN MONASTERY, AND LATER SERVED AS A TEXTILE FACTORY

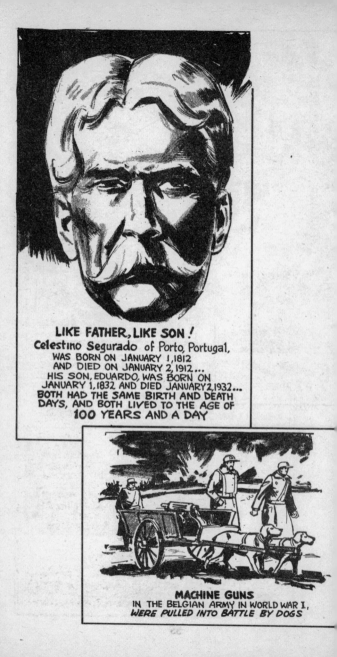

LIKE FATHER, LIKE SON !
Celestino Segurado of Porto, Portugal,
WAS BORN ON JANUARY 1,1812
AND DIED ON JANUARY 2, 1912...
HIS SON, EDUARDO, WAS BORN ON
JANUARY 1,1832 AND DIED JANUARY 2,1932...
BOTH HAD THE SAME BIRTH AND DEATH
DAYS, AND BOTH LIVED TO THE AGE OF
100 YEARS AND A DAY

MACHINE GUNS
IN THE BELGIAN ARMY IN WORLD WAR I,
WERE PULLED INTO BATTLE BY DOGS

THE **TOMBSTONE**
OF HEINRICH BRUGSCH,
THE FAMED
GERMAN
EGYPTOLOGIST,
IN THE CEMETERY
AT CHARLOTTENBURG,
GERMANY,
*ORIGINALLY
SERVED 6,000
YEARS EARLIER
IN GIZEH, EGYPT,
AS A COFFIN LID*

THE **OLD WINDMILL** of Nantucket, Mass.,
IS HELD TOGETHER ONLY WITH
WOODEN PINS, AND WAS BUILT
ENTIRELY FROM TIMBER SALVAGED
FROM WRECKED SHIPS

A **FEMALE FIGURE**
FASHIONED
FROM RYE,
IS PLACED IN
THE FIELDS OF
THE EISACK VALLEY
IN SO. TYROL,
*TO MAKE
CERTAIN THE
CORN WILL BE
FRUITFUL*

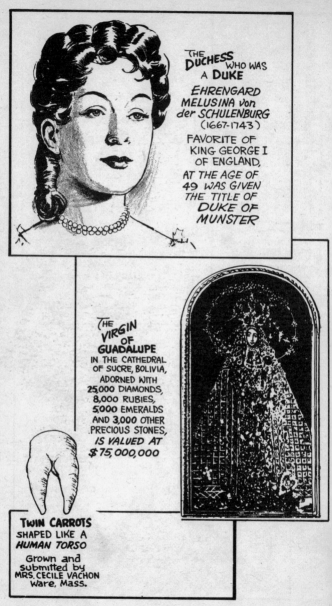

THE **DUCHESS** WHO WAS A **DUKE**

EHRENGARD MELUSINA von der SCHULENBURG (1667-1743) FAVORITE OF KING GEORGE I OF ENGLAND, AT THE AGE OF 49 WAS GIVEN THE TITLE OF *DUKE OF MUNSTER*

THE **VIRGIN** OF **GUADALUPE** IN THE CATHEDRAL OF SUCRE, BOLIVIA, ADORNED WITH 25,000 DIAMONDS, 8,000 RUBIES, 5,000 EMERALDS AND 3,000 OTHER PRECIOUS STONES, *IS VALUED AT $75,000,000*

TWIN CARROTS SHAPED LIKE A *HUMAN TORSO*

Grown and submitted by MRS. CECILE VACHON Ware, Mass.

THE RULER WHO CAN'T EVEN RISE FROM HIS CHAIR!

THE NYIMI OF THE BAKUBA TRIBE, IN THE CONGO, WEARS A CEREMONIAL COSTUME WEIGHING **220 POUNDS--**

SO LOADED WITH FURS, ANIMALS' TEETH AND BEADS, THAT HE CANNOT STAND UP!

HIS COSTUME IS NEARLY 4 TIMES THE WEIGHT OF THE HEAVIEST SUIT OF ARMOR WORN BY KNIGHTS OF OLD

BACK HOME

Epitaph OF WRITER IRVIN S. COBB IN OAK GROVE CEMETERY, PADUCAH, KY.

MARCANTONIO PACELLI
(1799 - 1902)
THE GRANDFATHER OF POPE PIUS XII,
LIVED IN 3 CENTURIES

JOVIAN'S COLUMN
IN ANKARA, TURKEY, HAS HAD A STORK'S NEST ATOP IT CONTINUOUSLY SINCE 365-- A PERIOD OF 1,610 YEARS

Mulkanundrakoorakooratarranina

SIGN
POINTING THE WAY TO AN AUSTRIAN VILLAGE

WITH A NAME CONTAINING 30 LETTERS

THE **ROCK OYSTER TOTEM POLE** in Saxman Totem Park, Alaska, COMMEMORATES A YOUNG TLINGIT INDIAN WHO WAS DROWNED BY A 15-FOOT TIDE BECAUSE HIS HAND WAS IN THE GRIP OF *A GIANT OYSTER*
Submitted by Emery F. Tobin Vancouver, Wash.

A **PISTOL** MADE IN GERMANY IN 1551, ALSO SERVED *AS AN AXE*

FORD RD
← AHEAD

NIXON RD
AHEAD →

SIGNPOST IN CHILLIWHACK, B.C.

Submitted by Randy Hawk, Athens, Ohio

SCHNURRSCH ERNST OF LANGENAUBACH, GERMANY, WAS SO PROUD OF HIS UMBRELLA THAT HE NEVER WENT ANY-WHERE WITHOUT IT -- AND WHEN IT RAINED HE IMMEDIATELY TOOK SHELTER SO IT WOULD NOT GET WET

THE LADY WHO WAS TRULY FIREPROOF

MADAME GIRADELLI AN ITALIAN PERFORMER IN THE EARLY 19th CENTURY, POURED MOLTEN LEAD INTO HER MOUTH, PASSED RED-HOT IRONS OVER HER BODY, LIMBS, TONGUE AND HAIR, THRUST HER HANDS INTO FIRE AND WASHED THEM **IN BOILING OIL**

THE **COAT-OF-ARMS** OF THE SCHWARZENBERG FAMILY IN ALL SAINTS' CHURCH, NEAR KUTNA HORA, CZECHOSLOVAKIA, IS A HUGE SHIELD *MADE FROM SEVERAL HUNDRED HUMAN BONES*

Submitted by
Emery F. Tobin,
Vancouver, Wash.

WILSON SHANNON
(1802-1877) SERVED SUCCESSIVELY AS GOVERNOR OF OHIO AND KANSAS

PHAGOCATA GRACILIS
A WATER CREATURE KNOWN AS A PLANARIAN, HAS 22 GULLETS -- EACH WITH ITS OWN MOUTH

AN ALL-EXPENSE TOUR TO EUROPE FOR A PERIOD OF 37 DAYS IN 1927, COST ONLY $385

THE HORSESHOE GATE
A GATEWAY IN TOLEDO, SPAIN, FEATURING THIS INSCRIPTION:
" I AM THE FINEST AND BEST PRESERVED GATEWAY IN THE CITY. THE MOORS BUILT ME EIGHT CENTURIES AGO, SHAPING THE PASSAGEWAY IN THE LIKENESS OF THEIR HORSES' HOOVES. THE KINGS FORTIFIED ME, THE SUN IS MY LOVER, GREETING ME EVERY MORNING AND TAKING LEAVE OF ME EVERY EVENING WITH A KISS; THEREFORE I AM KNOWN AS PUERTA DEL SOL -- THE GATEWAY OF THE SUN

PRESIDENT WARREN HARDING (1865-1923) 29th CHIEF EXECUTIVE, WAS A SCHOOL-TEACHER AT **16**

THE **DIVINE JARS** of **BORNEO** ARE WORSHIPED AS GODS BY THE DUSAN TRIBE

250-RUBLE NOTE ISSUED IN THE REPUBLIC OF SEMIRETSHYE (now part of Russia) IN 1918, WAS SECURED NOT BY GOLD, BUT BY A QUANTITY OF OPIUM CORRESPONDING IN VALUE TO THE NOTES ISSUED

"THE ROYAL WILLIAM" FIRST SHIP TO CROSS THE ATLANTIC UNDER CONTINUOUS STEAM, AFTER BEING SOLD TO SPAIN AND RENAMED THE "ISABELLA SEGUNDA," BECAME THE FIRST STEAM WARSHIP FROM WHICH A GUN WAS FIRED IN BATTLE

WILL PICKETT of Taylor, Texas, PERFORMING IN A RODEO IN CHEYENNE, WYOMING, IN 1904, THREW A STEER *BY BITING IT!*

THE CHURCH OF THE HOLY TRINITY

THE CHURCH OF THE HOLY TRINITY-- TORONTO, ONTARIO, WAS BUILT WITH 5,000 POUNDS CONTRIBUTED ANONYMOUSLY BY AN ENGLISHWOMAN WHO WAS DISMAYED TO LEARN THAT EXISTING CHURCHES IN TORONTO *RENTED PEWS TO PARISHIONERS*

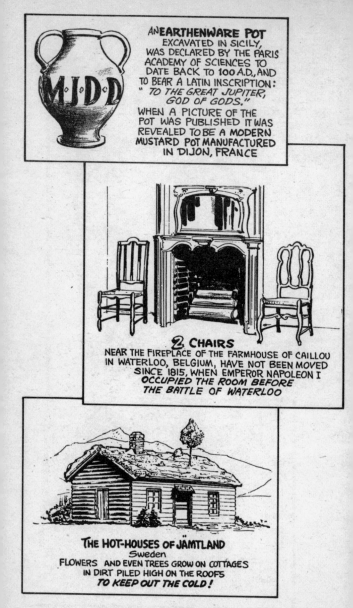

AN **EARTHENWARE POT**
EXCAVATED IN SICILY,
WAS DECLARED BY THE PARIS
ACADEMY OF SCIENCES TO
DATE BACK TO 100 A.D., AND
TO BEAR A LATIN INSCRIPTION:
" *TO THE GREAT JUPITER,
GOD OF GODS.*"
WHEN A PICTURE OF THE
POT WAS PUBLISHED IT WAS
REVEALED TO BE A MODERN
MUSTARD POT MANUFACTURED
IN DIJON, FRANCE

2 CHAIRS
NEAR THE FIREPLACE OF THE FARMHOUSE OF CAILLOU
IN WATERLOO, BELGIUM, HAVE NOT BEEN MOVED
SINCE 1815, WHEN EMPEROR NAPOLEON I
*OCCUPIED THE ROOM BEFORE
THE BATTLE OF WATERLOO*

THE HOT-HOUSES OF JÄMTLAND
Sweden
FLOWERS AND EVEN TREES GROW ON COTTAGES
IN DIRT PILED HIGH ON THE ROOFS
TO KEEP OUT THE COLD!

THE HORSE THAT COVERED 550 MILES IN 7½ DAYS!

"Paddy" A HORSE OWNED BY PIONEER SAM DALE (1772-1841), CARRIED DALE AND A VITAL MESSAGE FROM THE SECY. OF WAR TO GEN. JACKSON FROM GEORGIA TO NEW ORLEANS --*CUTTING SIX DAYS FROM THE NORMAL TRAVELING TIME*

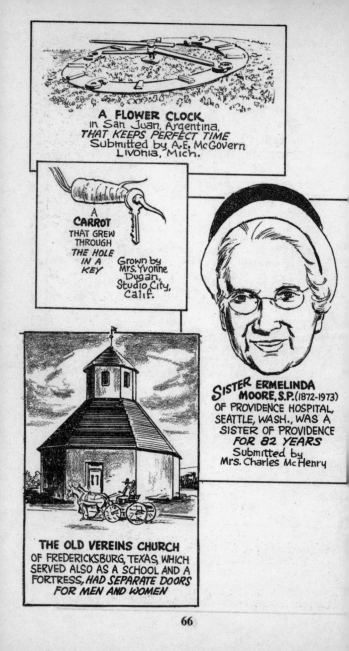

A FLOWER CLOCK
IN San Juan, Argentina,
THAT KEEPS PERFECT TIME
Submitted by A.E. McGovern
Livonia, Mich.

A CARROT
THAT GREW
THROUGH
*THE HOLE
IN A
KEY*
Grown by
Mrs. Yvonne
Dugan,
Studio City,
Calif.

**SISTER ERMELINDA
MOORE,** S.P. (1872-1973)
OF PROVIDENCE HOSPITAL,
SEATTLE, WASH., WAS A
SISTER OF PROVIDENCE
FOR 82 YEARS
Submitted by
Mrs. Charles McHenry

THE OLD VEREINS CHURCH
OF FREDERICKSBURG, TEXAS, WHICH
SERVED ALSO AS A SCHOOL AND A
FORTRESS, *HAD SEPARATE DOORS
FOR MEN AND WOMEN*

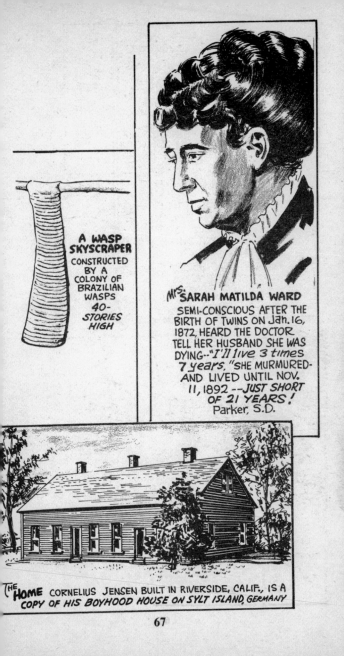

A WASP SKYSCRAPER CONSTRUCTED BY A COLONY OF BRAZILIAN WASPS *40-STORIES HIGH*

Mrs. SARAH MATILDA WARD SEMI-CONSCIOUS AFTER THE BIRTH OF TWINS ON Jan. 16, 1872, HEARD THE DOCTOR TELL HER HUSBAND SHE WAS DYING--*"I'll live 3 times 7 years,"* SHE MURMURED-- AND LIVED UNTIL NOV. 11, 1892--*JUST SHORT OF 21 YEARS!* Parker, S.D.

THE **HOME** CORNELIUS JENSEN BUILT IN RIVERSIDE, CALIF., IS A *COPY OF HIS BOYHOOD HOUSE ON SYLT ISLAND, GERMANY*

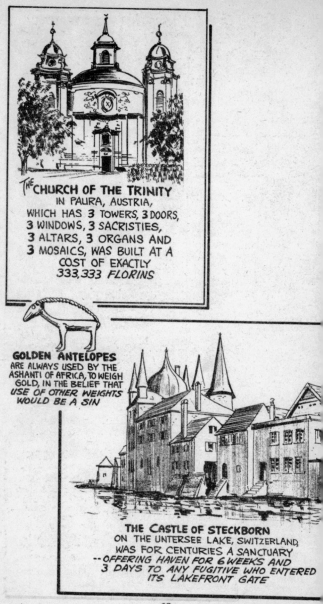

THE CHURCH OF THE TRINITY
IN PAURA, AUSTRIA,
WHICH HAS **3** TOWERS, **3** DOORS,
3 WINDOWS, **3** SACRISTIES,
3 ALTARS, **3** ORGANS AND
3 MOSAICS, WAS BUILT AT A
COST OF EXACTLY
333,333 FLORINS

GOLDEN ANTELOPES
ARE ALWAYS USED BY THE
ASHANTI OF AFRICA, TO WEIGH
GOLD, IN THE BELIEF THAT
*USE OF OTHER WEIGHTS
WOULD BE A SIN*

THE CASTLE OF STECKBORN
ON THE UNTERSEE LAKE, SWITZERLAND,
WAS FOR CENTURIES A SANCTUARY
--OFFERING HAVEN FOR 6 WEEKS AND
3 DAYS TO ANY FUGITIVE WHO ENTERED
ITS LAKEFRONT GATE

THE STRANGEST BOOK COLLECTOR IN ALL HISTORY!

JUAN VICENTE, A LIBRARIAN OF BARCELONA, SPAIN, MURDERED 9 PEOPLE BETWEEN 1830 AND 1835 --EACH TIME TO GAIN POSSESSION OF A SINGLE BOOK

DR. MANASSEH CUTLER (1742-1823) CLERGYMAN AND CONGRESSMAN FROM MASSACHUSETTS, WAS A DOCTOR OF LAW, A DOCTOR OF DIVINITY AND A DOCTOR OF MEDICINE

THE TWINS WHO LIVED IN DIFFERENT CENTURIES

François **AND** Etienne

GIRARD

WERE TWIN BROTHERS OF LYON, FRANCE;
BUT FRANCOIS WAS BORN ON DECEMBER 31, 1800
AND ETIENNE ON JANUARY 1, 1801,
AND THEY DIED IN DIFFERENT CENTURIES
-- *EACH PASSING AWAY ON HIS 100th BIRTHDAY*

THE **FENCE** AROUND FT. WASHINGTON, CAMBRIDGE, MASS.,
HAS POSTS IN THE SHAPE OF CANNON, AND
PICKETS RESEMBLING BATTLE-AXES AND SPEARS

YEAR-OLD PENGUINS ARE LARGER THAN THEIR PARENTS THEY HAVE THE COMPLETE ADULT PLUMAGE UNDER THEIR COAT OF DOWN--WHICH MAKES THEM BULKIER THAN ADULTS

THE HALLOWED COFFIN IN WHICH CALIPH MOKTAFI WAS BURIED, IN 1160, WAS MADE FROM THE ORIGINAL DOORS OF THE KAABAH, in Mecca *-THE MOST VENERATED SHRINE OF THE MOHAMMEDANS*

$$108 \sqrt{X} = 801$$

CAN YOU COMPLETE THE PROBLEM ON THIS TORN PIECE OF PAPER SO THAT THE RESULTANT NUMBER WILL BE THE EXACT REVERSE OF THE FIRST NUMBER? (TURN UPSIDE DOWN TO READ ANSWER BELOW)

THE RIVER THAT HAS A BED OF MARBLE The FIUM ALTO near Piedicroce, Corsica, FOR A DISTANCE OF 7 MILES HAS AS ITS BED A QUARRY THAT YIELDS A HIGHLY DESIRABLE GREEN MARBLE. *THE QUARRY CAN BE WORKED ONLY DURING THE SUMMER MONTHS WHEN THE RIVER IS SHALLOW*

$$1089 = 9 \times 6801$$
(ANSWER)

71

THE WIDOWS' WHIP

EVERY WOMAN OF THE ALGA TRIBE OF SO. ETHIOPIA UPON BECOMING A WIDOW MUST FLOG HERSELF WITH A SPECIAL TYPE OF LEATHER WHIP AS AN EXPRESSION OF HER GRIEF *EVERY DAY FOR 7 YEARS*

THE RUINED CASTLE

ON PEACOCK ISLAND, BERLIN, GERMANY, WAS NEVER AN ACTUAL CASTLE --HAVING BEEN CONSTRUCTED AS A RUIN IN 1797

MARY FEILDING

(1613 - 1638) WAS MARRIED TO THE FIRST DUKE OF HAMILTON *WHEN SHE WAS 7 YEARS OF AGE AND HER HUSBAND 14*

72

THE MUSIC WITH THE MOST TRAGIC SCORE IN OPERATIC HISTORY!

EUGENE MASSOL, TENOR STAR OF THE PARIS OPERA, AT THE PERFORMANCE OF "CHARLES VI" ON FEB. 9, 1849, SANG IN FRENCH THE LINE, "OH, GOD, CRUSH HIM," WITH A FINGER POINTING AT THE VAULTED CEILING *FROM WHICH AT THAT MOMENT A STAGEHAND FELL TO HIS DEATH!*
THE FOLLOWING NIGHT MASSOL POINTED TO AN EMPTY LOGE AS HE SANG THE LINE, BUT A PATRON ENTERED IT *--AND DROPPED DEAD!*
ON THE 3rd NIGHT THE TENOR GESTURED AT THE ORCHESTRA PIT *--AND A MUSICIAN COLLAPSED AND DIED!*
THE OPERA WAS NOT REVIVED UNTIL 1858, WHEN IT WAS TO HONOR EMPEROR NAPOLEON III, BUT ASSASSINS BOMBED THE EMPEROR'S PARTY *--CAUSING 156 CASUALTIES*

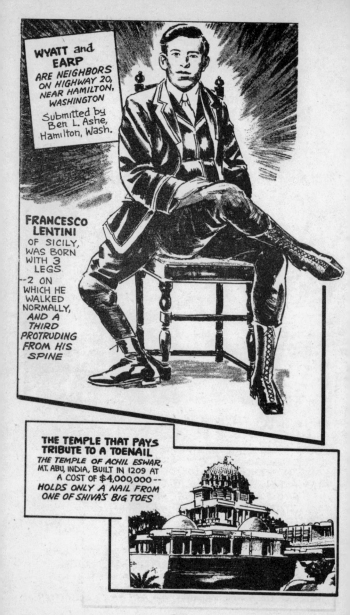

WYATT and EARP
ARE NEIGHBORS ON HIGHWAY 20, NEAR HAMILTON, WASHINGTON

Submitted by Ben L. Ashe, Hamilton, Wash.

FRANCESCO LENTINI
OF SICILY, WAS BORN WITH 3 LEGS. -2 ON WHICH HE WALKED NORMALLY, AND A THIRD PROTRUDING FROM HIS SPINE

THE TEMPLE THAT PAYS TRIBUTE TO A TOENAIL
THE TEMPLE OF ACHIL ESWAR, MT. ABU, INDIA, BUILT IN 1209 AT A COST OF $4,000,000 -- HOLDS ONLY A NAIL FROM ONE OF SHIVA'S BIG TOES

74

ALONSO TOSTADO (1400–1455) FAMED SPANISH AUTHOR, COULD ACCURATELY REPRODUCE ANY BOOK FROM MEMORY AFTER HAVING READ IT TWICE

MR. BURY IS AN UNDERTAKER in Ellenville, N.Y.

Submitted by MRS. HERBERT F. LOWN KINGSTON, N.Y.

THE **CHURCH OF NOTRE DAME** in Pouzanges, France, WAS PURCHASED DURING THE FRENCH REVOLUTION *BY 4 PRIVATE CITIZENS FOR $200* IT WAS RESTORED TO SERVICE 136 YEARS LATER WHEN THE DIOCESE REPURCHASED IT FROM 27 HEIRS OF THE 4 WHO HAD SAVED THE EDIFICE

75

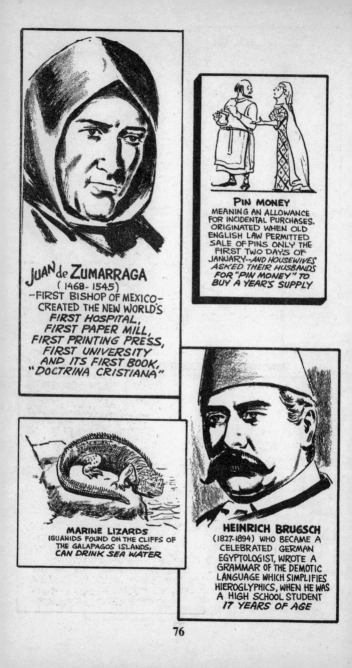

JUAN de ZUMARRAGA
(1468-1545)
–FIRST BISHOP OF MEXICO–
CREATED THE NEW WORLD'S
*FIRST HOSPITAL,
FIRST PAPER MILL,
FIRST PRINTING PRESS,
FIRST UNIVERSITY
AND ITS FIRST BOOK,
"DOCTRINA CRISTIANA"*

PIN MONEY
MEANING AN ALLOWANCE
FOR INCIDENTAL PURCHASES,
ORIGINATED WHEN OLD
ENGLISH LAW PERMITTED
SALE OF PINS ONLY THE
FIRST TWO DAYS OF
JANUARY--AND HOUSEWIVES
ASKED THEIR HUSBANDS
FOR "PIN MONEY" TO
BUY A YEAR'S SUPPLY

MARINE LIZARDS
IGUANIDS FOUND ON THE CLIFFS OF
THE GALAPAGOS ISLANDS,
CAN DRINK SEA WATER

HEINRICH BRUGSCH
(1827-1894) WHO BECAME A
CELEBRATED GERMAN
EGYPTOLOGIST, WROTE A
GRAMMAR OF THE DEMOTIC
LANGUAGE WHICH SIMPLIFIES
HIEROGLYPHICS, WHEN HE WAS
A HIGH SCHOOL STUDENT
17 YEARS OF AGE

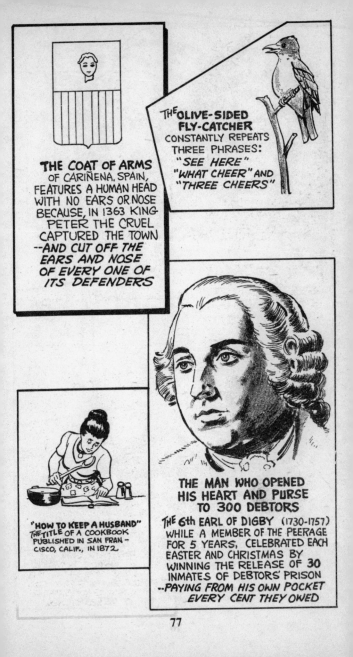

THE COAT OF ARMS OF CARIÑENA, SPAIN, FEATURES A HUMAN HEAD WITH NO EARS OR NOSE BECAUSE, IN 1363 KING PETER THE CRUEL CAPTURED THE TOWN --AND CUT OFF THE EARS AND NOSE OF EVERY ONE OF ITS DEFENDERS

THE **OLIVE-SIDED FLY-CATCHER** CONSTANTLY REPEATS THREE PHRASES: *"SEE HERE"* *"WHAT CHEER"* AND *"THREE CHEERS"*

"HOW TO KEEP A HUSBAND" THE TITLE OF A COOKBOOK PUBLISHED IN SAN FRANCISCO, CALIF., IN 1872.

THE MAN WHO OPENED HIS HEART AND PURSE TO 300 DEBTORS THE 6th EARL OF DIGBY (1730-1757) WHILE A MEMBER OF THE PEERAGE FOR 5 YEARS, CELEBRATED EACH EASTER AND CHRISTMAS BY WINNING THE RELEASE OF **30** INMATES OF DEBTORS' PRISON --PAYING FROM HIS OWN POCKET EVERY CENT THEY OWED

JOHN OF LORRAINE (1498-1550)
BECAME BISHOP OF METZ, FRANCE, AT THE AGE OF 7 --
HE BECAME A CARDINAL AT 20, AND HELD 12 BISHOPRICS AND WAS ABBOT OF 10 MONASTERIES

CURRENCY ONCE USED IN *SOME AREAS* OF THE FAR EAST, CONSISTED OF *COMPRESSED TEA BRICKS*

A **CLOTHES-PIN** INVENTED BY T.L. GOBLE IN THE 19th CENTURY, FEATURED A SLIDING-PEG THAT COULD TIGHTEN THE PIN'S GRIP

THE FIRST MOBILE HOMES HOUSES ON WHEELS, PULLED BY OXEN, WERE USED BY *AMERICAN PIONEERS WHO SETTLED THE WEST*

78

"THE MAN WITHOUT A COUNTRY" BY EDWARD EVERETT HALE, WAS INSPIRED BY THE LIFE OF CLEMENT L. VALLANDIGHAM, A CONGRESSMAN FROM OHIO, WHO BITTERLY OPPOSED THE CIVIL WAR AND AS A RESULT WAS DEPORTED FROM THE U.S. BY PRESIDENT LINCOLN. HALE WROTE "THE MAN WITHOUT A COUNTRY" SOLELY AS A MEANS OF DEFEATING VALLANDIGHAM IN HIS ABSENTEE CAMPAIGN TO BE ELECTED GOVERNOR OF OHIO

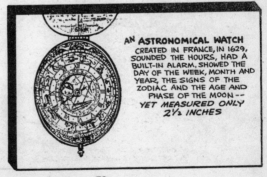

AN **ASTRONOMICAL WATCH** CREATED IN FRANCE, IN 1629, SOUNDED THE HOURS, HAD A BUILT-IN ALARM, SHOWED THE DAY OF THE WEEK, MONTH AND YEAR, THE SIGNS OF THE ZODIAC AND THE AGE AND PHASE OF THE MOON -- *YET MEASURED ONLY 2½ INCHES*

A 2-STORY FARM-HOUSE NEAR BROKEN BOW, NEBR., MADE WITH SOD WALLS --AT A TOTAL COST OF $500

THE MAN WHO WAS KILLED BY HIS OWN BEARD! Hans Steininger of Braunau, Austria, WAS FATALLY INJURED FALLING DOWN A FLIGHT OF STAIRS IN 1567 WHEN HE TRIPPED OVER HIS OWN WHISKERS! HIS BEARD WAS OVER 8 FEET IN LENGTH

THE STRANGEST WEDDINGS IN ALL HISTORY!

RAJAH SHIVAJI of Tanjore, India,
UNHAPPY BECAUSE HE HAD NO MALE HEIR,
TOOK 17 WIVES IN A SINGLE DAY!

HE MARRIED 9 GIRLS IN ONE CEREMONY AND 8 MORE THE
SAME EVENING – YET HE DIED WITHOUT A MALE HEIR,
AND THE EAST INDIA COMPANY SEIZED HIS STATE (1855)

MONTICELLO
THOMAS JEFFERSON'S HOME NEAR CHARLOTTESVILLE, VA., WAS
DESIGNED BY JEFFERSON WITH A BILLIARD ROOM IN ITS DOME
*-- BUT BEFORE THE HOUSE WAS FINISHED
VIRGINIA OUTLAWED BILLIARDS*

A **FRENCH TRAVELING CLOCK**
CREATED MORE THAN 200 YEARS AGO,
CAME WITH ITS OWN CARRYING CASE

CORPSES OF THE IGOROTS OF THE PHILIPPINES,
ONCE WERE LEFT EXPOSED ON A MOUNTAIN TOP
UNTIL THE HOT SUN HAD MUMMIFIED THEM

PAUL REVERE (1735-1818) THE FAMED SILVERSMITH AND HERO OF LONGFELLOW'S POEM, WAS ALSO A DENTIST AND MADE HIS HISTORIC RIDE ON A *BORROWED HORSE THAT WAS NEVER RETURNED TO ITS OWNER*

THE CASTLE OF BEVILLIERS-BRETEUIL in France, HAS BEEN OCCUPIED BY THE SAME FAMILY *FOR 366 YEARS*

THE **STRANGE PROPHECY OF THE SEA** —
Boscombe, England, Dec. 26, 1852
THE "WILLIAM GLEN ANDERSON," A BARK DRIVEN
ASHORE IN A STORM, WAS WRECKED NEAR A
THEATER IN WHICH THE PLAY BEING ENACTED
WAS *"THE WRECK ASHORE"*

A **COUNTY COURTHOUSE**
MEASURING 48' BY 52',
WAS MOVED FROM HEMINGFORD TO
ALLIANCE, NEB., A DISTANCE OF 19 MILES,
BALANCED ON A RAILROAD TRAIN (1899)

STONE
THAT LOOKS LIKE
THE FACE OF A FOX
Submitted by
Kenneth Kunzen,
Seven Hills, Ohio

A
**MINIATURE
SILVER
SKIFF**
DISPLAYED IN
THE CHURCH OF
TINOS, GREECE,
IS A REPLICA OF AN ACTUAL
BOAT THAT WAS STOVE IN
--BUT WHICH WAS SAVED FROM SINKING
WITH ITS CREW WHEN A LARGE FISH
BECAME WEDGED IN THE BROKEN KEEL

A **DRINKING HORN** FOUND AT GALLEHUS, DENMARK, AND USED 2,500 YEARS AGO, IS SOLID GOLD

THE **GENERAL** WHO HONORED HIS FAMILY NAME BY MARRYING 5 TIMES!

GEN. ALEXANDRE MALOT (1754-1821)

4 TIMES A WIDOWER, SUCCESSIVELY MARRIED 5 WOMEN NAMED:

MARGUERITE,
ANNE,
LOUISE,
OTTILIE and
TERESE

AL **COUTURE** of Lewiston, Maine, IN A BOXING MATCH WITH RALPH WALTON, KNOCKED OUT HIS OPPONENT IN 10½ SECONDS
-Sept. 24, 1946-

THE **MONASTERY OF THE CONCEPTIONISTS**
in Agreda, Spain,
WHICH TOOK 7 YEARS TO CONSTRUCT,
WAS BEGUN IN 1643 WHEN ITS BUILDERS
HAD A TOTAL CAPITAL OF ONLY 12 REALES
-- *THE EQUIVALENT OF 60 CENTS*

THE IRON MAN !
ALEXANDER ZASS
A POLISH STRONG MAN KNOWN AS
" THE AMAZING SAMSON"
PERMITTED HIMSELF TO BE RUN OVER
*BY AN AUTOMOBILE CARRYING
12 PASSENGERS*

THE **WILD CORNEL**
IN ITS
EARLY
STAGE OF
BLOOMING
ENVELOPS
ITS FLOWERS
IN A
" BASKET "

THE
**GINKGO
TREE**
OLDEST
OF ALL TREES,
*FIRST
APPEARED
ON EARTH
200,000,000
YEARS AGO*

A *CUTTER* OWNED BY DAVID KANOA, OF TARAWA, IN THE GILBERT ISLANDS, CAPTURED BY THE JAPANESE IN 1941, TOWED TO SEA AND BOMBED, DRIFTED WITHOUT A HAND ON ITS WHEEL FOR 12 MONTHS, AND FINALLY FOUND ITS WAY BACK TO ITS HOME PORT--PENETRATING A NARROW, HAZARDOUS CHANNEL

HERE LIES JANE SMITH
WIFE OF THOMAS SMITH,
MARBLE CUTTER
MONUMENTS OF THE SAME
STYLE 350 DOLLARS

Epitaph in Springdale Cemetery, Ohio

THE *SITE* OF THE ENTIRE VILLAGE OF ST. ANNES, LANCASHIRE, ENGLAND, WAS LEASED BY ITS OWNER TO A COMPANY IN 1875, FOR A PERIOD OF 1,100 YEARS

CAPT. PETER MATHIESON (1871-1954) BECAUSE HE WAS BORN ABOARD A SHIP OFF GRAVESEND, ENGLAND, DIRECTED THAT UPON HIS DEATH HIS BODY WAS TO BE CREMATED, AND *HIS ASHES SCATTERED OVER THE SEA*

THE **PALM MODEL** A REVOLVER MADE IN 1895 COULD BE CONCEALED IN THE PALM OF ONE HAND AND *WAS FIRED BY SQUEEZING THE GRIP*

THE NATIONAL CATHEDRAL in Washington, D.C., WAS CONSTRUCTED TO DUPLICATE IN SIZE AND HEIGHT *KING SOLOMON'S TEMPLE IN JERUSALEM, BUILT 3,000 YEARS AGO*

THE ROYAL GUARDSMEN WHO THOUGHT THEY COULD BAR THEIR GATE TO DEATH!

QUEEN ANNE (1665-1714) OF ENGLAND WAS ASSIGNED A SMALL ARMY OF GUARDS AT HER LONDON PALACE IN A DESPERATE ATTEMPT TO PROTECT HER CHILDREN--- *YET ALL 17 DIED BEFORE THEIR MOTHER-* THE GUARDS EXCLUDED EVERY STRANGER --BUT ALWAYS OPENED THE GATE TO THE MILKMAN WHOSE UNPASTEURIZED MILK BROUGHT DEATH

THE **VIRGIN AND CHILD** *NATURAL STALAGMITE FORMATION* CAVE OF THE FAIRIES, LANGUEDOC, FRANCE

A **MEDAL** COINED IN 1677 BY CHRISTIAN WILHELM KROHNEMANN, A GERMAN ALCHEMIST, BEARS AN INSCRIPTION STATING *THAT ITS GOLD WAS MADE FROM BASE METAL.* KROHNEMANN WAS PROVEN A FRAUD AND HANGED

A **WINGLESS FLY** ONLY HALF AN INCH LONG *IS ANTARCTICA'S LARGEST LAND ANIMAL*

PIERRE GASSENDI (1592-1655) WAS A PROFESSOR OF RHETORIC AT THE UNIVERSITY OF DIGNE, FRANCE, IN 1608, AT THE AGE OF *16*

THE BALANCING SQUATTER OF BENARES
AN INDIAN HOLY MAN AT THE FEAST OF
TREEMIRI, IN BENARES, INDIA,
BALANCES FOR DAYS ON A
SINGLE WOODEN SANDAL

CHAIR
MADE FROM
TIMBERS OF SIR
FRANCIS DRAKE'S
*"THE GOLDEN
HIND"*
Presented to
Oxford Univ.
in 1662, and
still preserved

**OLD
STONE
FACE**
FAEROE
ISLANDS,
NATURAL
ROCK
SCULP-
TURE

THE MOST AMAZING PLAYWRIGHT IN HISTORY!
Gerardo Lobo (1610-1668) POET AT THE COURT OF KING PHILIP IV OF SPAIN, COULD CREATE A 3-ACT PLAY ON ANY SUBJECT AND RECITE IT ENTIRELY IN RHYME-- A 3-HOUR IMPROVISATION

THE SIGN OF FRIENDSHIP AFFIXED ON PERSONAL LETTERS FROM THE MOGUL EMPERORS OF INDIA, WAS AN IMPRESSION OF THE MONARCH'S HAND

THE **PÁI LÙ** AN ORNAMENTAL GATE IN CHUFU, CHINA, BEARS THE INSCRIPTION: "Gate of the eternal spring which will last 10,000 generations"

I WAS BORN 199 YEARS TOO SOON!

A **MARRIAGE LICENSE** in Orange County, N.C., IN 1776, COST $75

THE **BELFRY** OF THE PARISH CHURCH OF MUNDINGEN, GERMANY, FORMERLY WAS ATTACHED TO THE MAURICIUS CHAPEL — *WHICH STOOD 30 MILES AWAY*

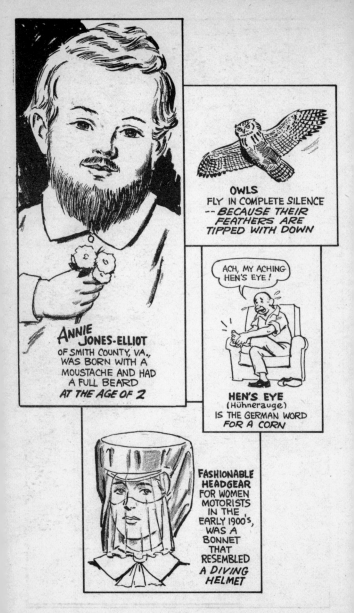

ANNIE JONES-ELLIOT OF SMITH COUNTY, VA., WAS BORN WITH A MOUSTACHE AND HAD A FULL BEARD *AT THE AGE OF 2*

OWLS FLY IN COMPLETE SILENCE -- *BECAUSE THEIR FEATHERS ARE TIPPED WITH DOWN*

ACH, MY ACHING HEN'S EYE!

HEN'S EYE (Hühnerauge) IS THE GERMAN WORD *FOR A CORN*

FASHIONABLE HEADGEAR FOR WOMEN MOTORISTS IN THE EARLY 1900's, WAS A BONNET THAT RESEMBLED A *DIVING HELMET*

NATURAL STONE BRIDGE NEAR LILECE, BULGARIA, FORMED BY MOUNTAIN STREAMS

STOOL CARVED BY THE IBOS OF NIGERIA FROM A SOLID BLOCK OF WOOD

TEDDY ROOSEVELT WHILE PRESIDENT OF THE UNITED STATES, AND AS VICE PRESIDENT AND AS GOVERNOR OF NEW YORK, STILL FOUND TIME TO READ 2 OR 3 BOOKS EACH DAY

O SILENT GRAVE TO THEE I TRUST
THE PRECIOUS PILE OF WORTHY DUST
KEEP IT SAFE O SACRED TOMBE
UNTIL A WIFE SHOULD ASK FOR ROOM

Epitaph of Solomon Farr in Longford, Tasmania

THE **CASTLE OF FLOBECQ** - France - WAS COMPLETELY RENOVATED IN 1939, BUT CAREFULLY PRESERVED IN ITS FAÇADE *ARE 3 BULLETS FIRED AT THE CHATEAU DURING THE FRENCH REVOLUTION*

THE **JOHN SHERMAN**," A SIDE-WHEELER STEAMSHIP, WAS BUILT AS A U.S. REVENUE CUTTER, REBUILT AS A PASSENGER STEAMER, AND *CONVERTED AFTER TWO YEARS INTO A BARGE*

THE DOWRY THAT CAME FROM A DEATH WISH !

DANIELE MORVAN of Pornic, France, ORPHANED, AND JILTED BY HER FIANCÉ BECAUSE SHE HAD NO DOWRY, LEAPED INTO THE OCEAN AND SANK TO THE BOTTOM 3 TIMES BEFORE SHE WAS RESCUED.

REVIVED, SHE WAS FOUND TO BE CLUTCHING SAND FROM THE OCEAN FLOOR--AND IN THE SAND WAS A $2,000 RUBY!

– 1881 –

HERE LIES THE BODY OF BETTY BODEN WHO WOULD HAVE LIVED LONGER BUT SHE CO'DEN

Epitaph IN WREXHAM CHURCHYARD, ENGLAND

97

THE BANK THAT WAS SENT BY MAIL
THE BANK OF VERNAL, UTAH, WAS BUILT FROM BRICKS SENT IN 50-POUND PACKAGES 427 MILES FROM SALT LAKE CITY, UTAH, BY PARCEL POST   (1916)
Submitted by Ralph B. Williams, Juneau, Alaska

THE GREAT BUDDHA OF TODAIJI TEMPLE, IN NARA, JAPAN, BUILT IN THE 8th CENTURY, CONTAINS 438 TONS OF COPPER, 2 TONS OF MERCURY AND 880 POUNDS OF GOLD— THE GOLD ALONE HAS A VALUE TODAY OF $2,032,800

TWIN ANIMAL HEADS NATURAL STONE FORMATION Bornholm Island, Denmark

STEPPING STONES STILL VISIBLE IN ANCIENT POMPEII, PERMITTED PEDESTRIANS TO CROSS WATER AND GARBAGE-FILLED STREETS. *THEY WERE PLACED WIDE ENOUGH APART TO ALLOW THE PASSAGE OF CHARIOT WHEELS*

THE POET WHO WALKED 28,000 MILES TO PROCLAIM HIS FAITH!

SA'DI (1184-1291) THE PERSIAN POET MADE 14 PILGRIMAGES FROM BAGHDAD TO MECCA BEFORE HIS DEATH AT THE AGE OF 107. *EACH TIME WALKING 2,000 MILES*

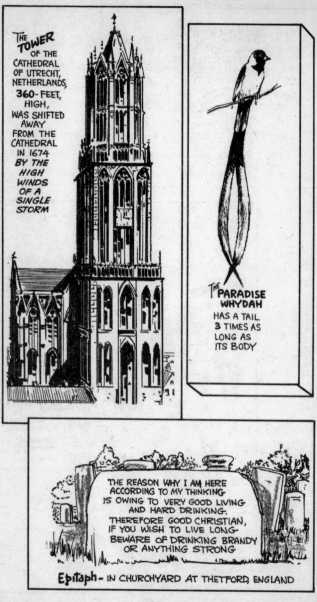

THE **TOWER** OF THE CATHEDRAL OF UTRECHT, NETHERLANDS, **360-FEET** HIGH, WAS SHIFTED AWAY FROM THE CATHEDRAL IN 1674 *BY THE HIGH WINDS OF A SINGLE STORM*

THE **PARADISE WHYDAH** HAS A TAIL **3** TIMES AS LONG AS ITS BODY

THE REASON WHY I AM HERE
ACCORDING TO MY THINKING
IS OWING TO VERY GOOD LIVING
AND HARD DRINKING.
THEREFORE GOOD CHRISTIAN,
IF YOU WISH TO LIVE LONG
BEWARE OF DRINKING BRANDY
OR ANYTHING STRONG

Epitaph – IN CHURCHYARD AT THETFORD, ENGLAND

A **WOMAN** OF THE BANGONGO TRIBE, AFRICA, IS PERMITTED TO WEAR A HORN-SHAPED HAIRDO -- NORMALLY RESERVED ONLY FOR THE CHIEF -- *AS A SIGN SHE IS EXPECTING HER FIRST CHILD*

OLD STONE FACE Poplar Lake, Ontario, *NATURAL ROCK FORMATION* Submitted by EMERY F. TOBIN, Vancouver, Wash.

JOHANN RUDOLF ZWINGER (1692-1777) TAUGHT LOGIC, ANATOMY AND BOTANY AT THE UNIVERSITY OF BASEL, SWITZERLAND, FOR 65 YEARS

THE **SENECIO PLANT** FOUND HIGH IN THE MOUNTAINS OF EAST AFRICA, IS PROTECTED FROM THE COLD BY ITS DEAD LEAVES *WHICH FORM A PROTECTIVE COVERING AROUND ITS STALK*

THE **OLDEST CLERGYMAN**

THE REV. C.F.L. L'OSTE OF Pyengana, Tasmania, LIVED TO THE AGE OF **107**

THE **DUK-DUK** OF NEW BRITAIN, AN ISLAND OFF NEW GUINEA, WHO IS A COMBINATION POLICEMAN, JUDGE AND HANGMAN, *CONCEALS HIS IDENTITY BEHIND A MASK AND A CLOAK OF LEAVES*

BED BUG INN
IONE, CALIFORNIA, A 20-ROOM HOTEL THAT WAS BUILT IN GOLD RUSH DAYS WHEN THE TOWN WAS NAMED BED BUG, *STILL USES THAT NAME*
Submitted by Jules H. Marr, Albuquerque, N.M.

THE SQUARE GOLD COINS MINTED BY KING FREDERICK II OF DENMARK IN 1563, WERE SO VEHEMENTLY OBJECTED TO BY HIS SUBJECTS, THAT THE MONARCH MADE REFUSAL TO ACCEPT THE COINS A CRIME

THE CHURCH OF SANTA MARIA MAGGIORE
NEAR MANFREDONIA, ITALY,
IS THE ONLY STRUCTURE REMAINING OF THE
TOWN OF SIPONTUM--*ABANDONED BY ITS
INHABITANTS 719 YEARS AGO*

A **POT** RESTING IN A FORKED STICK IS CONSIDERED SACRED BY NATIVES OF DAHOMEY, AFRICA, WHO BELIEVE THAT IF THE POT SHOULD FALL THE *ENTIRE UNIVERSE WOULD COLLAPSE*

THE **HAJI BAIRAM MOSQUE** IN ANKARA, TURKEY, WAS BUILT AS A PAGAN TEMPLE--WAS CONVERTED INTO A CHRISTIAN CHURCH IN 500 A.D. --*AND BECAME A MOSQUE 575 YEARS AGO*

JAY HAMMOND
of South Naknek, Alaska,
BECAME GOVERNOR OF THAT STATE
*BY DEFEATING EVERY FORMER
GOVERNOR IN ITS HISTORY*
Submitted by Flip Todd,
Anchorage, Alaska

THE FASCES
THE
ANCIENT
ROMAN
SYMBOL OF UNITY,
GAVE MUSSOLINI
THE NAME OF HIS
FASCIST PARTY

A SINGLE TREE
STANDS IN THE CENTER OF THE TENERE WASTE
-- A 600-MILE AREA OF THE SAHARA --
YET, ONCE THE ENTIRE COUNTRY WAS
COVERED WITH LUXURIANT VEGETATION

THE MAN WHO FRIGHTENED OFF A LION -- *WITH A BICYCLE!*

KENNETH KAUNDA FOUNDER AND PRESIDENT OF ZAMBIA, ONCE DROVE AWAY A MENACING LION BY LIFTING UP THE BICYCLE HE HAD BEEN RIDING AND *BRANDISHING IT AS A WEAPON!*

HAUSTORIUS
A SAND-BURROWING AMPHIPOD *ALWAYS SWIMS UPSIDE DOWN*

THE MAN WHO WAS NEVER ILL IN **114 YEARS!** FRANCESCO HUZZAPOLI (1587-1702) OF CASALE, ITALY, HAD HIS FIRST ILLNESS IN THE LAST YEAR OF HIS LIFE, AND *MARRIED FOR THE 5th TIME AT 98!* HIS WHITE HAIR TURNED BLACK AT THE AGE OF **100** AND HIS BEARD AND EYEBROWS TURNED BLACK AT **112**

THE STONE HOUSES OF SELIME, TURKEY, ARE BUILT INTO A MOUNTAIN'S NATURAL CONES OF SOLID ROCK

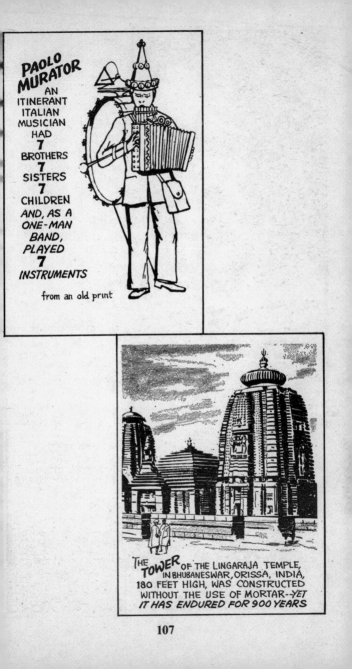

PAOLO MURATOR AN ITINERANT ITALIAN MUSICIAN HAD **7** BROTHERS **7** SISTERS **7** CHILDREN AND, AS A ONE-MAN BAND, PLAYED **7** INSTRUMENTS

from an old print

THE **TOWER** OF THE LINGARAJA TEMPLE, IN BHUBANESWAR, ORISSA, INDIA, 180 FEET HIGH, WAS CONSTRUCTED WITHOUT THE USE OF MORTAR—YET IT HAS ENDURED FOR 900 YEARS

A MAN ON THE ISLAND OF ONTONG JAVA, IN THE SOLOMONS, ANNOUNCES THE BIRTH OF HIS FIRST CHILD *BY CUTTING TWO SLITS IN THE TIP OF HIS NOSE, AND INSERTING IN THEM A LARGE ORNAMENT MADE OF TURTLE SHELLS*

A CUP PRESENTED IN 1666 TO THE CITY OF FRANKFORT ON THE MAIN, GERMANY, BY MATHIAS BANSA AS A BRIBE TO HELP HIM OBTAIN A LICENSE TO OPEN AN APOTHECARY SHOP, IS MADE FROM THE HORN OF THE NARWHAL, *LONG BELIEVED TO HAVE MAG- ICAL MEDICAL VALUES*

WINGED MONSTER near Ogrodzieniec, Poland, *NATURAL ROCK FORMATION*

108

LIPICAN HORSES ARE BORN WITH A BLACK MANE AND TAIL *WHICH TURN WHITE AFTER 3 TO 7 YEARS*

THE BELFRY OF ST. PETER'S CHURCH IN TACOMA, WASH., WAS THE MAMMOTH TRUNK OF A FIR TREE, *SUPPORTING ATOP IT THE CHURCH BELL*

CAT WITH THE OUTLINE OF A MOTH ON ITS SIDE Submitted by Deirdra Marcyan, San Diego, Cal.

JOHN WILKES A MEMBER OF THE BRITISH PARLIAMENT, WAS OUTLAWED FOR CRITICIZING KING GEORGE III --BUT LATER BECAME LORD MAYOR OF LONDON

OAK LEAF MEASURING 14" BY 8½"

Submitted by Linda C. Walker, Moore, S.C.

FISH IN THE POOLS SURROUNDING THE MOSQUES OF THE MANANGKABAU, INDONESIA, ARE CONSIDERED SACRED, AND BECOME SO TAME *THEY CAN BE FED BY HAND*

MARGARET FULLER (1810-1850), THE FIRST FEMALE NEWSPAPER REPORTER, CRITIC AND EDITOR OF A DISTINGUISHED LITERARY PUBLICATION, *COULD READ LATIN AT THE AGE OF 6*

THE **FIRST HEAVY TRUCK** in Masterton, N.Z., HAD 4 SOLID HARD TIRES EACH 10 INCHES THICK--AND *IT TOOK 48 HOURS TO MOUNT THEM ON THE WHEELS*

A CEDAR OF LEBANON TREE GROWING IN FRONT OF THE ROYAL CASTLE IN BAD HOMBURG, GERMANY, WAS THE ENGAGEMENT GIFT PRESENTED TO HIS SISTER BY THE DUKE OF CAMBRIDGE *155 YEARS AGO*

THE **HOMES** OF NATIVES OF THE BISSAGOS ISLANDS OF WEST AFRICA, ARE BUILT AROUND LARGE TREES-- WITH THE TRUNK PROVIDING THE MAIN SUPPORT, AND *BRANCHES AND THEIR LEAVES, THE ROOF*

A WAR MEMORIAL IN LAPPEENRANTA, FINLAND, IS A MILESTONE THAT WAS PIERCED BY RUSSIAN CANNONBALLS *IN THE WAR OF 1741*

THE **ONLY ROUND BOOK IN THE WORLD** ITS COVERS FOLD BACK AT THE MIDDLE-- MADE BY BOOK-BINDER KASPAR MEUSER FOR THE GERMAN COURT OF SAXONY IN THE *16th CENTURY*

THE SURFER WHO RODE A TIDAL WAVE!

Holoua, A RESIDENT OF KAUAI, HAWAII, WHEN A TIDAL WAVE SWEPT HIS HOME OUT TO SEA IN 1868, TORE A PLANK FROM THE WALL OF THE HOUSE, AND RODE A 50-FOOT WAVE BACK TO SHORE

MECHANICAL SINGING BIRD
CONSTRUCTED BY AN EGYPTIAN INVENTOR NAMED HERO *2,000 YEARS AGO* THE BIRD SITS ON AN AIRTIGHT TANK AND SINGS WHEN WATER IS POURED INTO THE TANK THROUGH A FUNNEL VALVE

113

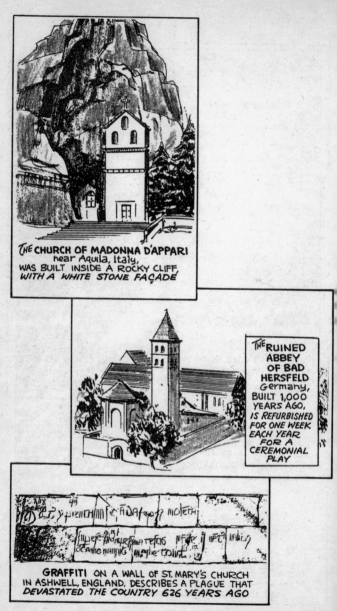

THE CHURCH OF MADONNA D'APPARI
near Aquila, Italy,
WAS BUILT INSIDE A ROCKY CLIFF,
WITH A WHITE STONE FAÇADE

THE RUINED ABBEY OF BAD HERSFELD Germany, BUILT 1,000 YEARS AGO, IS REFURBISHED FOR ONE WEEK EACH YEAR FOR A CEREMONIAL PLAY

GRAFFITI ON A WALL OF ST. MARY'S CHURCH
IN ASHWELL, ENGLAND, DESCRIBES A PLAGUE THAT
DEVASTATED THE COUNTRY 626 YEARS AGO

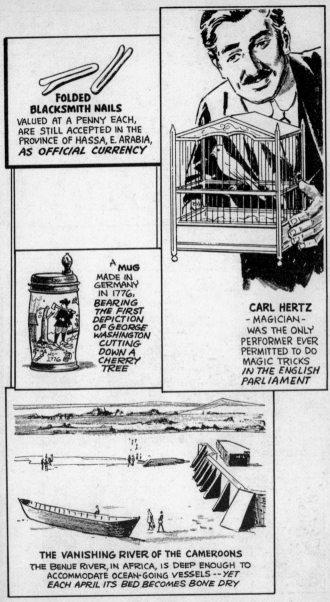

FOLDED BLACKSMITH NAILS
VALUED AT A PENNY EACH, ARE STILL ACCEPTED IN THE PROVINCE OF HASSA, E. ARABIA, *AS OFFICIAL CURRENCY*

A **MUG** MADE IN GERMANY IN 1776, BEARING *THE FIRST DEPICTION OF GEORGE WASHINGTON CUTTING DOWN A CHERRY TREE*

CARL HERTZ
– MAGICIAN –
WAS THE ONLY PERFORMER EVER PERMITTED TO DO MAGIC TRICKS *IN THE ENGLISH PARLIAMENT*

THE VANISHING RIVER OF THE CAMEROONS
THE BENUE RIVER, IN AFRICA, IS DEEP ENOUGH TO ACCOMMODATE OCEAN-GOING VESSELS -- *YET EACH APRIL ITS BED BECOMES BONE DRY*

FRED B. NOBLE WAS AWARDED AN EARNED MASTER'S DEGREE IN HISTORY AT JACKSONVILLE UNIV., FLA., ON *HIS 91st BIRTHDAY*

A **BLACK DUCK** SHOT AT GOOSE BAY, VT., BY RAYMOND F. LAVALLEY OF SO. BURLINGTON, VT., HAD BEEN BANDED *13 YEARS AND 4 MOS. EARLIER*

THE **ANTLERS** OF A FULL-GROWN BULL MOOSE *WEIGH MORE THAN 60 POUNDS*

3 CHURCHES IN ALTÖTTING, BAVARIA-- THE LOCAL ABBEY, THE CHURCH OF THE JESUITS AND THE CHURCH OF THE HOLY CHAPEL, *STAND SIDE BY SIDE*

116

THE **ROYAL KITCHEN** OF THE MARBLE PALACE IN POTSDAM, GERMANY, IS LOCATED BESIDE THE CASTLE-- *DISGUISED AS A RUINED PAGAN TEMPLE*

THE **SALT-WATER CROCODILES** of Ceylon, OFTEN GROW TO A LENGTH OF 22 FEET, *AND WEIGH MORE THAN 1,600 POUNDS*

THE CHURCH OF SANTA MARIA IN COSMEDIN IN ROME, IN ANCIENT TIMES, WAS A CORN WAREHOUSE SERVING *NEEDY CITIZENS OF THE ROMAN EMPIRE*

117

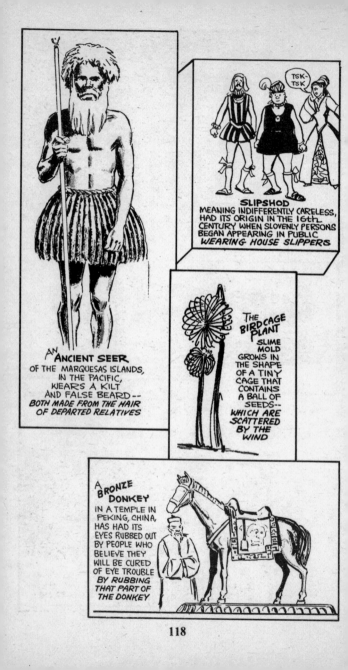

TSK-TSK

SLIPSHOD
MEANING INDIFFERENTLY CARELESS, HAD ITS ORIGIN IN THE 16th CENTURY WHEN SLOVENLY PERSONS BEGAN APPEARING IN PUBLIC *WEARING HOUSE SLIPPERS*

AN **ANCIENT SEER**
OF THE MARQUESAS ISLANDS, IN THE PACIFIC, WEARS A KILT AND FALSE BEARD-- *BOTH MADE FROM THE HAIR OF DEPARTED RELATIVES*

THE **BIRDCAGE PLANT**
SLIME MOLD GROWS IN THE SHAPE OF A TINY CAGE THAT CONTAINS A BALL OF SEEDS-- *WHICH ARE SCATTERED BY THE WIND*

A **BRONZE DONKEY**
IN A TEMPLE IN PEKING, CHINA, HAS HAD ITS EYES RUBBED OUT BY PEOPLE WHO BELIEVE THEY WILL BE CURED OF EYE TROUBLE *BY RUBBING THAT PART OF THE DONKEY*

118

BRISTLE-CONE PINES IN THE WHITE MOUNTAINS OF CALIF., ARE 4,000 YEARS OLD

THE POPPING STONE
IS THE NAME GIVEN TO A ROCK AT GILSLAND, SCOTLAND, ON WHICH SIR WALTER SCOTT, THE NOVELIST, "POPPED THE QUESTION" TO HIS SWEETHEART, CHARLOTTE CARPENTER

ST. JAMES' OLD CATHEDRAL
in Melbourne, Australia, WAS DISASSEMBLED IN 1914, AND REBUILT WITH THE SAME STONES IN ANOTHER PART OF THE CITY

THE **SPIT** IN COLONIAL AMERICA'S KITCHENS, OFTEN WAS TURNED BY A *DOG RUNNING ON A TREADMILL*

A **CLIMBING PLANT** IS GROWN AT THE CONVENT OF ST. CATHERINE, ON MOUNT SINAI, *AS A MEMORIAL TO THE BURNING BUSH MENTIONED IN EXODUS 3:2*

THE **WAR MEMORIAL** of Bailleul, France, IS THE RUIN OF THE TOWN CHURCH--DESTROYED BY WORLD WAR I BOMBS

A **RED PEPPER** *WITH A GREEN PEPPER GROWING INSIDE IT.*

Submitted by GRACE D. CRAGG, Masonville, N.J.

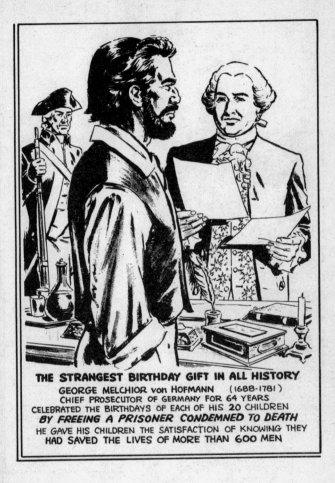

THE STRANGEST BIRTHDAY GIFT IN ALL HISTORY
GEORGE MELCHIOR von HOFMANN (1688-1781)
CHIEF PROSECUTOR OF GERMANY FOR 64 YEARS
CELEBRATED THE BIRTHDAYS OF EACH OF HIS 20 CHILDREN
BY FREEING A PRISONER CONDEMNED TO DEATH
HE GAVE HIS CHILDREN THE SATISFACTION OF KNOWING THEY
HAD SAVED THE LIVES OF MORE THAN 600 MEN

CHARLES PAUL de KOCK
(1794-1871), WHO BECAME A CELEBRATED
FRENCH NOVELIST AND PLAYWRIGHT,
SAVED HIS MOTHER'S LIFE
5 MONTHS BEFORE HE WAS BORN!
HIS FATHER WAS EXECUTED DURING THE
FRENCH REVOLUTION, BUT HIS MOTHER WAS
SPARED AND LIVED FOR ANOTHER 60 YEARS

KEY RINGS
FASHIONABLE IN ANCIENT ROME, HAD USABLE KEYS PROJECTING FROM THEM

THE **TOADSTOOL GRAIN BINS OF ANGOLA** Africa — GRAIN IS SAFEGUARDED FROM CHICKENS AND WILD ANIMALS BY PACKING IT INTO LARGE GRASS BAGS *WHICH ARE SECURED ATOP TALL POSTS*

LINCOLN STEFFENS (1866-1936) AMERICAN AUTHOR AND LECTURER, WROTE IN A MINUTE, ALMOST INDECIPHERABLE SCRIPT TO CONCEAL THE FACT THAT HE WAS A *POOR SPELLER*

THE MILKWEED BUTTERFLY HAS A SENSE OF SMELL 100 TIMES STRONGER THAN THAT OF A *BLOODHOUND*

THE SANTA FOSCA CHURCH
ON TORCELLO ISLAND, VENICE, ITALY
WAS BUILT IN THE 12TH CENTURY AS A REPLICA OF
THE CHURCH OF SANTA SOPHIA, IN CONSTANTINOPLE

LOUISE MADELINE PITTMAN OF ATLANTA, GA., AT THE AGE OF 17, IN 1936, DECIDED TO DIVIDE HER TIME BETWEEN 2 SETS OF PARENTS *BECAUSE A HOSPITAL MIX-UP WHEN SHE WAS BORN MADE IT IMPOSSIBLE TO DETERMINE HER REAL MOTHER*

A **CASTLE** IN SUSA, IRAN, BUILT BY FRENCH ARCHAEOLOGISTS FROM ANCIENT BRICKS AND COLUMNS FOUND IN *RUINS 2,000 YEARS OLD*

A **STONE HEAD** IN SUORVA, LAPLAND, LOOKS LIKE THE TIN MAN IN THE WIZARD OF OZ

THE **FIRST AMERICAN-BORN NOVELIST** *CHARLOTTE LENNOX* (1720-1804) WHO PUBLISHED "LIFE OF HARRIOT STUART" IN 1750, WAS BORN IN NEW YORK CITY

THE **BIRD OF PREY** NEAR LEBAUX, FRANCE, *NATURAL ROCK FORMATION*

THE **BELFRY** OF THE CHURCH OF DERDINGEN, GERMANY, WAS CONSTRUCTED ON THE *ROOF OF AN INHABITED NEIGHBORING HOME*

MATCHES USED IN THE U.S. IN 1840, COULD BE IGNITED AT *EITHER END*

HOMES ON THE ISLAND OF SANTORIN, IN THE AEGEAN SEA, *ARE BUILT INTO A ROCKY CLIFF*

SILK PURSE MADE IN BOSTON, MASS., *FROM SOWS' EARS*

THE ENTRANCE TO ST. PAUL'S CHURCH, DAMASCUS, SYRIA, ONCE SERVED AS THE CITY WALL'S GATE, OVER WHICH *THE APOSTLE WAS LOWERED IN A BASKET TO ELUDE PURSUERS*

"THE WASHINGTON POST MARCH" ONE OF JOHN PHILIP SOUSA'S MOST POPULAR MARCHES, SOLD MORE THAN 1,000,000 COPIES IN 5 YEARS-- YET IT NETTED HIM ONLY $35

ST. DOMINIC SAVIO (1842-1857) WHO WAS CANONIZED IN 1954, WAS A SCHOOLBOY OF MURIALDO, ITALY, WHEN HE DIED AT THE AGE OF 15

THE TOMBSTONE OF AN ANCIENT ROMAN TOOLMAKER, IN OSTIA, ITALY, DEPICTS HIS SHOP AND ALL THE TOOLS OF HIS TRADE

BOSTON, MASSACHUSETTS, IS A CITY IN WHICH BACK BAY IS ALL DRY LAND ... DOCK SQUARE HAS NO SEA NOR DOCK ... FORT HILL SQ. HAS NO FORT NOR HILL ... AND SCHOOL STREET HAS NO SCHOOL ...

Submitted by Emery F. Tobin, Vancouver, Wash.

THE MAN WHO COULD DO ANYTHING! WILLIAM BARNES (1801-1886) AN ENGLISH SCHOOLTEACHER, WAS ALSO AN ACCOMPLISHED POET, DRAFTSMAN MECHANIC, ENGRAVER, MATHEMATICIAN, CLOCKMAKER, CARPENTER, GARDENER, LUTE PLAYER, VIOLINIST, PIANIST, ARCHAEOLOGIST, AND SPOKE 62 LANGUAGES

THE OLD AGE HOME in Nuremberg, Germany, WHICH SPANS THE RIVER PEGNITZ, WAS ORIGINALLY BUILT AS A HOSPITAL IN **1331**

EXCAVATIONS ON THE SITE OF AN OLD WAPPATO INDIAN VILLAGE ON THE COLUMBIA RIVER, NEAR WARREN, ORE., IN AN AREA OF LESS THAN 225 BY 50 FT., *YIELDED 13,481 ARROWHEADS* Submitted by Emery F. Tobin, Vancouver, Wash.

AN ANCIENT COLUMN near Vraserca, Greece, IS NOW USED AS A DRINKING TROUGH FOR **SHEEP**

THE **CHURCH OF THE ASSUMPTION** in Caprafico, Italy, WAS CONSTRUCTED IN THE 15th CENTURY, *ON A SITE SELECTED BY A GOAT...*

THE GOAT WAS ALLOWED TO ROAM FREELY, AND THE CHURCH WAS BUILT WHERE IT STOPPED TO EAT FROM A FIG TREE

THE MOST DEDICATED PILGRIMS IN THE WORLD
Mount Minobu, Japan

BUDDHISTS PAYING HOMAGE AT THE GRAVE OF NICHIREN
FOUNDER OF A JAPANESE SECT,
REMAIN MOTIONLESS AND SILENT WHILE
5 CANDLES PLACED ON EACH OUTSTRETCHED ARM
BURN DOWN INTO THEIR FLESH

THE HIPPOPOTAMUS TREE NATURAL FORMATION ON A WHITE OAK IN THE MISSOURI OZARKS
Submitted by Emery F. Tobin, Vancouver, Wash.

ADMIRAL SIR PETER PARKER COMMANDING A FLEET OF 10 WARSHIPS, FIRED 7,000 CANNON-BALLS AT THE FORT GUARDING CHARLESTON HARBOR, IN 1776, YET THERE WERE ONLY 36 AMERICAN CASUALTIES

A SUNBURST DAHLIA WITH 2 PETALS GROWING OUT OF ITS CENTER
Submitted by Mary Beth Wolf, Oshkosh, Wisc.

A ROYAL STATUE OF EGYPTIAN PHARAOH RAMSES II HAS BEEN LYING UNFINISHED IN THE GRANITE QUARRIES OF ASWAN, EGYPT, FOR MORE THAN 3,200 YEARS

130

WIDOWS

IN SOME PARTS OF GREECE ARE RESPECTED IN THEIR MOURNING BY NEVER PERMITTING LEVITY IN THEIR PRESENCE FOR A PERIOD OF 2 YEARS

THE WHITE BELLBIRD OF SO. AMERICA, CAN BE HEARD MORE THAN A MILE AWAY

THE TREE THAT GROWS IN A DUNGEON
Scotland.
A HAWTHORN TREE HAS FLOURISHED IN THE DUNGEON OF CAWDOR CASTLE FOR **521** YEARS.
ACTING ON A DREAM, ITS OWNER LOADED HIS TREASURE CHEST ON A DONKEY, AND BUILT HIS CASTLE, IN 1454, AROUND THE TREE -- BECAUSE THAT IS WHERE THE ANIMAL PAUSED TO GRAZE

DANTE, Cape Manerba, Italy,
NATURAL STONE PROFILE OF THE ITALIAN AUTHOR

THE **BOLBOCERAS BEETLE** of Australia, SOUNDS LIKE A WHINING PUPPY

THE **STONE FLOWER-POT** - Hopewell, New Brunswick

THE CROWN
AN INN IN CHIDDINGFOLD, ENGLAND,
WAS USED AS A BREWERY IN THE 14th CENTURY-
FOR A RENTAL OF LESS THAN $1 A YEAR

A BOAT
ON THE BEACH OF BLANES, SPAIN,
HAS REMAINED UNFINISHED FOR 60 YEARS

THE FIRST AMBULANCES
HORSE-DRAWN 2-WHEEL CARTS EQUIPPED WITH
SPRINGS, WERE INVENTED BY BARON DOMINIQUE JEAN
LARREY, NAPOLEON'S PERSONAL SURGEON, IN **1792**

A CONVERTIBLE "CUPBOARD"
USED SHORTLY AFTER THE CIVIL WAR,
THAT OPENED UP TO BE A DOUBLE BED --
WITH A LOWER BERTH THAT SERVED AS A CRIB

A **POPLAR** near Ude, Mongolia,
IS ONE OF ONLY 3 TREES IN THE ENTIRE GOBI DESERT
--AN AREA OF 500,000 SQ. MILES

**EVERY
METAL
UTENSIL**
USED BY THE ADI TRIBE OF INDIA,
ALSO SERVES AS CURRENCY, WITH THE
HIGHEST DENOMINATION A **METAL CAULDRON**

THE**HUMAN
BRIDGE**
ALEXANDER ZASS - A PROFESSIONAL STRONGMAN
CALLED *"THE AMAZING SAMSON,"* SUPPORTED ON HIS CHEST
A DOUBLE RAMP HOLDING 25 MEN

John Paul Jones

WAS AN ALIAS ADOPTED BY THE HERO OF THE AMERICAN REVOLUTION WHO FLED SCOTLAND BECAUSE UNDER HIS REAL NAME OF JOHN PAUL, *HE HAD BEATEN ONE MURDER CHARGE, AND FACED A SECOND*

4,000 POUNDS OF ROSES ARE REQUIRED IN BULGARIA TO PRODUCE *1 POUND OF ATTAR*

DR. ARTHUR LUTZE of Anhalt-Cöthen, Germany, WHO CLAIMED TO BE A "WONDER-HEALER," WAS GRANTED PERMISSION BY THE RULING DUKE OF ANHALT-CÖTHEN, IN 1854, TO PRINT 71,000 IN THALERS HIMSELF TO FINANCE CONSTRUCTION OF A SANITARIUM

135

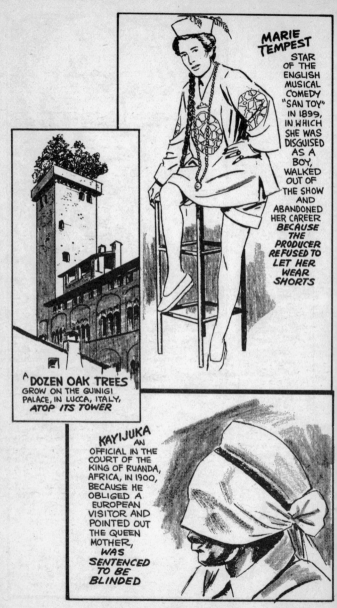

MARIE TEMPEST STAR OF THE ENGLISH MUSICAL COMEDY "SAN TOY" IN 1899, IN WHICH SHE WAS DISGUISED AS A BOY, WALKED OUT OF THE SHOW AND ABANDONED HER CAREER *BECAUSE THE PRODUCER REFUSED TO LET HER WEAR SHORTS*

A **DOZEN OAK TREES** GROW ON THE GUINIGI PALACE, IN LUCCA, ITALY, *ATOP ITS TOWER*

KAYIJUKA AN OFFICIAL IN THE COURT OF THE KING OF RUANDA, AFRICA, IN 1900, BECAUSE HE OBLIGED A EUROPEAN VISITOR AND POINTED OUT THE QUEEN MOTHER, *WAS SENTENCED TO BE BLINDED*

THE MARINER WHO DESTROYED AN ENTIRE ENEMY FLEET SINGLEHANDEDLY

PAOLO di CASSIA, AN ITALIAN SEAMAN, WHOSE FIANCÉE, MIRELLA, WAS KIDNAPED BY TURKISH PIRATES, USED AN AIR BLADDER IN 1547 TO SWIM UNDERWATER FOR SEVERAL HUNDRED YARDS TO WHERE A TURKISH FLEET OF **50** GALLEYS WAS ANCHORED, AND WITH HEMP, SULPHUR AND EXPLOSIVES *BLEW UP THE ENTIRE FLEET*—

AT THE SOUND OF THE EXPLOSIONS, MIRELLA LEAPED INTO THE WATER FROM THE CASTLE TOWER IN WHICH SHE WAS BEING HELD AND HER FIANCÉ RESCUED HER UNHARMED

THE HERO WHOSE REWARD FOR SAVING FRANCE WAS LIFE IMPRISONMENT

JACQUES CASSARD (1672-1740)
TWICE SAVED FRANCE FROM DISASTROUS FAMINES
BY EQUIPPING WARSHIPS AT HIS OWN EXPENSE
TO CONVOY GRAIN SHIPS, ROUTED ENGLISH RAIDERS
AND CAPTURED 18 ENGLISH VESSELS ...
YET WHEN HE REQUESTED REIMBURSEMENT
FOR HIS EXPENSES, HE WAS IMPRISONED IN
THE FORTRESS OF HAM, DYING IN HIS CELL
10 YEARS LATER

THE HOUSES IN A VILLAGE IN THE HOGGAR AREA
OF THE SAHARA DESERT, ARE HUGE ROCKS --
HOLLOWED OUT TO PROVIDE SHELTER

THE **TEBELDI TREE**
of the Sudan, Africa, IS USED BY NATIVES AS A RESEVOIR-- *STORING WATER IN THE HOLLOW TRUNK*

MOTHER BERNARDA MORIN (1832-1929) CANADIAN-BORN FOUNDER OF THE SISTERS OF PROVIDENCE IN CHILE, *CREATED 22 CONVENTS THERE AND WAS A NUN FOR 78 YEARS*

A MONUMENT
IN DEAD HORSE GULCH, IN THE SAWTOOTH MOUNTAINS, ALASKA, PAYS TRIBUTE TO: " *3,000 PACK ANIMALS THAT LAID OUR BONES ON THESE AWFUL HILLS DURING THE GOLD RUSH OF 1897-98* "

Submitted by EMERY F. TOBIN, Vancouver, Wash.

THE MANDRILL · BABOON
AS AN ADULT HAS
BLUISH CHEEKS AND A
BRIGHT RED NOSE

THE FAMINE SPRING
IN OKERKOCHEN, GERMANY,
IS SO NAMED BECAUSE IT
PROVIDES WATER ONLY IN YEARS
*WHEN THERE HAS BEEN
A CROP FAILURE*

SIGNATURE
OF THE
DAKOTA
INDIAN
CHIEF
*SITTING
BULL*

THE CHURCH OF NOTRE DAME de fin des **TERRES**
IN SOULAC-SUR-MER, FRANCE, BUILT IN THE 10th
CENTURY, WAS EXCAVATED IN 1859, AFTER HAVING
*BEEN BURIED UNDER SAND DUNES
FOR 106 YEARS*

140

THE LOVE THAT MOVED AN ENTIRE VILLAGE

CASTELLAR, A COMMUNITY OF 29 HOUSES IN THE FRENCH ALPS, WAS SHIFTED FROM ONE MOUNTAIN PEAK TO ANOTHER, IN 1435, AT THE REQUEST AND EXPENSE OF HENRI LASCARIS -- *SO THE GIRL HE LOVED WOULD BE NEARER TO HIM*

Epitaph IN THE LUSHAI HILLS OF BURMA, ON THE GRAVE OF BACHA, A HUNTING DOG THAT KILLED *405 DEER AND 150 OTHER ANIMALS*

IN MEMORY OF
BACHA
OF THAWNGLIANA'S VILLAGE
THE CLEVEREST HOUND
IN THE WORLD

PAPER MONEY ISSUED IN DENOMINATIONS AS LOW AS 50 CENTS BY PRIVATE BANKS AND EVEN INDIVIDUALS IN THE UNITED STATES IN THE 1840's, WERE SO VALUELESS *THEY WERE CALLED "SHINPLASTERS"*

PATAPSCO SAVINGS FUND,
FIFTY CENTS

A GREEK VASE

DEPICTED IN A PAINTING IN THE BERLIN MUSEUM, REVEALS THAT THE ANCIENTS SPUN YO-YOS IN 700 B.C.

THE ACHATIUS CHAPEL IN GRÜNSFELDHAUSEN, GERMANY, BUILT IN THE 12th CENTURY, WAS HALF BURIED IN RIVER MUD UNTIL 1803

WATERMELON WEIGHING 197 POUNDS" Grown by Edward E. Weeks, Tarboro, N.C.

THE ALCAZAR in Toledo, Spain, HAS BEEN BURNED TO THE GROUND 9 TIMES

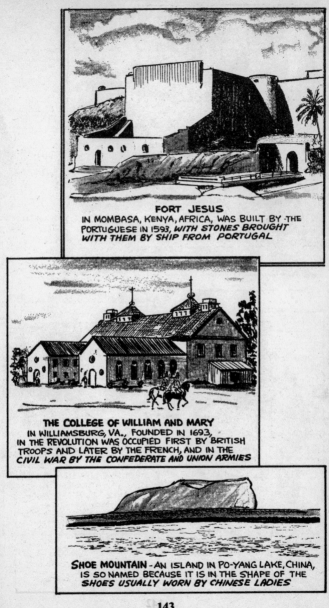

FORT JESUS
IN MOMBASA, KENYA, AFRICA, WAS BUILT BY THE
PORTUGUESE IN 1593, *WITH STONES BROUGHT
WITH THEM BY SHIP FROM PORTUGAL*

THE COLLEGE OF WILLIAM AND MARY
IN WILLIAMSBURG, VA., FOUNDED IN 1693,
IN THE REVOLUTION WAS OCCUPIED FIRST BY BRITISH
TROOPS AND LATER BY THE FRENCH, AND IN THE
CIVIL WAR BY THE CONFEDERATE AND UNION ARMIES

SHOE MOUNTAIN — AN ISLAND IN PO-YANG LAKE, CHINA,
IS SO NAMED BECAUSE IT IS IN THE SHAPE OF THE
SHOES USUALLY WORN BY CHINESE LADIES

THE CAVE VILLAGE of Alamazora, Spain, IN WHICH EVERY FAMILY ONCE LIVED IN CAVERNS, HAS BEEN ABANDONED EXCEPT FOR ONE FAMILY *STILL OCCUPYING A CAVE AT THE FOOT OF THE MOUNTAIN*

QUEEN ANNE (1664-1714), of England, WAS THE MOTHER OF 17 CHILDREN -- ONLY ONE OF WHOM LIVED BEYOND INFANCY

THE WATER WORKS AT BETHLEHEM, PA., WHICH BEGAN OPERATION ON JUNE 27, 1755, *WAS AMERICA'S FIRST PUBLIC UTILITY*

THE **MURDER** THAT WAS REVEALED BY A DREAM!
PRIVATE JOHN GIVEN
of Company B, 22 nd Virginia Regiment,
ON HIS WAY HOME FOR A FURLOUGH ON MAY 7, 1862,
WAS SLAIN BY MARAUDING UNION SOLDIERS
WHO BURIED HIS BODY—
SEVERAL DAYS LATER HIS WIFE SAW THE
KILLING REENACTED IN A DREAM—AND LED
POLICE STRAIGHT TO HER HUSBAND'S BODY!

FOOT STOVES
HEATED BY CHARCOAL,
WERE USED IN AMERICA
IN THE 1800's
*IN CHURCHES,
IN SLEIGHS AND
STAGECOACHES*

THE TOUCAN
HAS AN ENORMOUS
RAINBOW-HUED BEAK--
YET THE BEAK WEIGHS
ONLY ABOUT ONE OUNCE

THE **CLUBS** USED BY THE NOOTKA INDIANS OF
VANCOUVER TO KILL SEALS WERE ALWAYS
WHITTLED IN THE SHAPE OF A SEAL

U.S. OIL WELLS
ONLY 6 YEARS AFTER THE FIRST DISCOVERY OF OIL IN 1859,
EXPORTED 30,000,000 GAL. OF CRUDE OIL AND OIL PRODUCTS

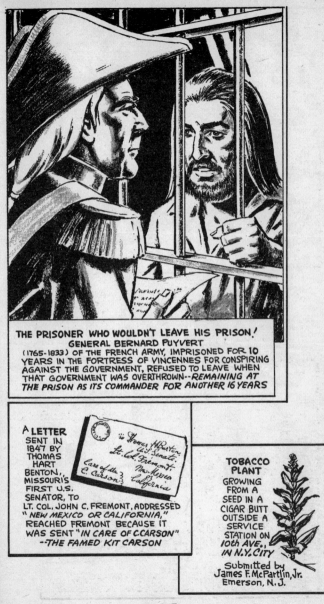

THE PRISONER WHO WOULDN'T LEAVE HIS PRISON!
GENERAL BERNARD PUYVERT
(1765-1833) OF THE FRENCH ARMY, IMPRISONED FOR 10
YEARS IN THE FORTRESS OF VINCENNES FOR CONSPIRING
AGAINST THE GOVERNMENT, REFUSED TO LEAVE WHEN
THAT GOVERNMENT WAS OVERTHROWN--*REMAINING AT*
THE PRISON AS ITS COMMANDER FOR ANOTHER 16 YEARS

A LETTER SENT IN 1847 BY THOMAS HART BENTON, MISSOURI'S FIRST U.S. SENATOR, TO LT. COL. JOHN C. FREMONT, ADDRESSED "NEW MEXICO OR CALIFORNIA," REACHED FREMONT BECAUSE IT WAS SENT "IN CARE OF C.CARSON" --THE FAMED KIT CARSON

TOBACCO PLANT GROWING FROM A SEED IN A CIGAR BUTT OUTSIDE A SERVICE STATION ON 10th AVE., IN N.Y. CITY

Submitted by James F. McPartlin, Jr. Emerson, N. J.

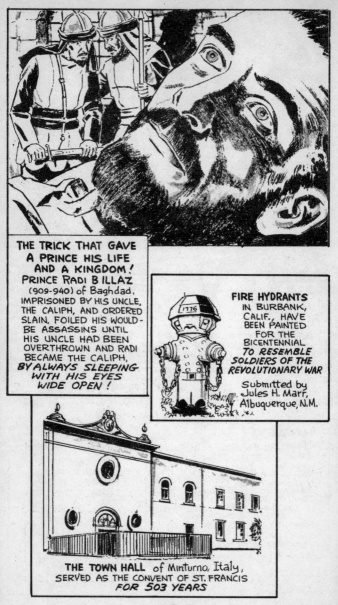

THE TRICK THAT GAVE A PRINCE HIS LIFE AND A KINGDOM!
PRINCE RADI BILLAZ (909-940) of Baghdad, IMPRISONED BY HIS UNCLE, THE CALIPH, AND ORDERED SLAIN, FOILED HIS WOULD-BE ASSASSINS UNTIL HIS UNCLE HAD BEEN OVERTHROWN AND RADI BECAME THE CALIPH, *BY ALWAYS SLEEPING WITH HIS EYES WIDE OPEN!*

FIRE HYDRANTS IN BURBANK, CALIF., HAVE BEEN PAINTED FOR THE BICENTENNIAL *TO RESEMBLE SOLDIERS OF THE REVOLUTIONARY WAR*

Submitted by Jules H. Marr, Albuquerque, N.M.

1776

THE TOWN HALL of Minturno, Italy, SERVED AS THE CONVENT OF ST. FRANCIS *FOR 503 YEARS*

THE FORTRESS OF PALAMIDI -GREECE-
IS REACHED BY 999 STEPS

DR. DAVID L. BERNIE of Dayton, Ohio, IS THE FATHER OF 5 SONS AND A DAUGHTER-- ALL OF THEM DOCTORS

CAN YOU ADD SIX 1's AND OBTAIN 12?

SOLUTION: $11 + \frac{11}{11} = 12$

149

THE HOMES OF THE CAPSIKI TRIBE OF THE CAMEROONS, AFRICA, ARE SHAPED LIKE HUGE WICKER WINE BOTTLES —EVEN TO THE CORK

THE PROBOSCIS MONKEY of Borneo, HAS A LONG PINK NOSE

SINGING FROGS in Japan, ARE KEPT IN CAGES BECAUSE THEY CHIRP SO SWEETLY

THE FIRST AIRCRAFT OF THE U.S. ARMY WAS A DIRIGIBLE BOUGHT IN 1908 — BUT IT WAS NEVER USED BECAUSE ONLY ITS INVENTOR, T.S. BALDWIN, WAS DARING ENOUGH TO FLY IT

SANGAY VOLCANO in Central Ecuador, HAS ERUPTED ALMOST CONTINUOUSLY *FOR MORE THAN 400 YEARS*

FRACTIONS AND A REGULAR DECIMAL SYSTEM WERE USED BY THE ANCIENT CRETANS WHO NOTED THE FIGURE 3252¾ THIS WAY:

◇◇◇ || °°°)) ∨∨∨

HIEROGLYPHICS OF THE ANCIENT HITTITES WHO DOMINATED ASIA MINOR FROM 1900 TO 1200 B.C., ARE READ FROM RIGHT TO LEFT ON ONE LINE, AND FROM LEFT TO RIGHT ON THE NEXT LINE

MATTHEW BRADY FAMED AMERICAN CIVIL WAR PHOTOGRAPHER, LOST MOST OF HIS PRICELESS PHOTOS IN 1875 BECAUSE *HE COULD NOT PAY A WAREHOUSE STORAGE CHARGE*

A U.S. ARMY SURGEON WHO NEVER WENT TO MEDICAL SCHOOL, WROTE A CLASSIC BOOK ON THE DIGESTIVE PROCESS--BASED ON OBSERVING A PATIENT *THROUGH A STOMACH WOUND THAT REFUSED TO HEAL FOR 7 YEARS*

THE DEATH-BED SCENE THAT ENABLED A QUEEN TO GET AWAY WITH MURDER!

QUEEN LAODICE, INCENSED BECAUSE KING ANTIOCHUS II OF SYRIA HAD BEEN UNFAITHFUL TO HER, POISONED THE MONARCH AND THEN REPLACED HIM ON HIS DEATH BED WITH AN ACTOR NAMED ARTEMON, WHO RESEMBLED THE KING SO CLOSELY HE WAS ABLE, IN HIS "LAST WORDS," TO ENJOIN THE COURT TO FOREVER HOLD THE QUEEN IN REVERENCE.

QUEEN LAODICE SPIRITED THE ACTOR OUT OF THE CASTLE, BURIED THE MURDERED MONARCH – AND KEPT HER CRIME SECRET AS LONG AS SHE LIVED (247 B.C.)

DANCING CARROTS

Submitted by
DAVE SHEILD
White Bear Lake,
Minnesota

THE CONE HOMES OF CAPPADOCIA TURKEY, ROCK CONES CREATED BY A NOW EXTINCT VOLCANO, AND OCCUPIED BY TURKISH FARMERS, *WERE HOLLOWED OUT AS CELLS AND CHAPELS BY EARLY CHRISTIANS AND HAVE AS MANY AS 10 FLOORS*

WHALES
WEIGHING 195 TONS, DEVELOP FROM THE SAME SIZE EGGS AS MICE

THE THICK-BILLED CUCKOO
HAS A CRY THAT SOUNDS LIKE " OUI, YES, YES "--
--A "YES MAN" IN 2 LANGUAGES

JAMES FENIMORE COOPER (1789-1851) FAMED FOR WRITING THE LEATHERSTOCKING TALES, ALSO WROTE "THE PILOT"-- *FIRST SEA STORY BY AN AMERICAN*

BULLOCKS PLOWING IN BALI, INDONESIA, WEAR HUGE DRUMS FILLED WITH STONES IN THE BELIEF THAT THE NOISE WILL *MAKE THEM MOVE FASTER*

SWORDS CARRIED BY GERMAN KNIGHTS IN THE 17th CENTURY, OFTEN HAD A WATCH IN THEIR HILT

A "CATENTAIL" OFFSPRING OF A CAT AND A RABBIT-- Submitted by MRS. ROBERT ZARLING, KEWASKUM, WISCONSIN

155

FAKED ACCIDENTS
WERE DISPLAYED IN REIGATE, ENGLAND,
AS A WARNING TO SPEEDING MOTORISTS --
WITH OVERTURNED CARS AND SMASHED "BODIES"

THE FIRST MECHANICAL CALCULATOR
WAS INVENTED BY
BLAISE PASCAL (1623-1662),
FOR USE IN HIS FATHER'S
TAX OFFICE IN ROUEN, FRANCE,
*WHEN PASCAL WAS STILL
IN HIS TEENS*

HORACE GREELEY
EDITOR OF THE OLD NEW YORK TRIBUNE, WROTE SO ILLEGIBLY THAT A REPORTER ONCE USED A DISMISSAL NOTE FROM HIM AS A *LETTER OF RECOMMENDATION*

THE BICENTENNIAL CLOCK

A GRANDFATHER'S CLOCK IN THE STATE DEPARTMENT, WASHINGTON, D.C., THAT STILL KEEPS TIME AND ALSO PLAYS 5 DIFFERENT MUSICAL SELECTIONS, WAS BUILT ENTIRELY BY HAND BY THOMAS HARLAND OF NORWICH, CONN., IN **1776**
Submitted by JULES H. MARR,
Albuquerque, N.M.

NATHANAEL GREENE

ENLISTED IN THE RHODE ISLAND MILITIA IN 1774 AS A PRIVATE, AND IN THE SPRING OF 1775 *WAS MADE COMMANDER OF THE TROOPS RAISED TO AID MASSACHUSETTS AT THE SIEGE OF BOSTON*

HAMMERFEST ON KVALOY ISLAND, NORWAY, *IS THE NORTHERNMOST CITY IN THE WORLD*

THE WAR OF THE KING'S WHISKERS

KING LOUIS VII (1121–1180)
RECEIVED A DOWRY OF 2 FRENCH PROVINCES
UPON HIS MARRIAGE TO ELEANOR, DAUGHTER
OF A FRENCH DUKE IN 1152, BUT WHEN HE
SHAVED OFF HIS BEARD AFTER THE WED-
DING, ELEANOR DIVORCED HIM, MARRIED
KING HENRY II OF ENGLAND, AND
DEMANDED RETURN OF THE DOWRY!

TO REGAIN THE PROVINCES, KING HENRY
DECLARED WAR ON FRANCE, AND THE
FIGHTING CONTINUED FOR 301 YEARS

2 MISSOURI BEARS
PRESENTED TO PRESIDENT
THOMAS JEFFERSON
BY ZEBULON PIKE,
WERE KEPT FOR A TIME ON
THE WHITE HOUSE LAWN

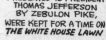

158

THE FIRST U.S. AIR FORCE WAS MANNED BY CIVILIANS
THE BALLOON CORPS OF THE UNION ARMY HAD SOLDIERS WORKING AS MAINTENANCE MEN, *BUT ITS FLYER-OBSERVERS WERE CIVILIANS*

BATH WAGONS
IN PARIS, FRANCE, IN THE EARLY 1900'S, WERE PULLED THROUGH THE STREETS *CARRYING A BATHTUB FOR TEMPORARY USE IN HOMES*

THE **WHITE HOUSE** IN WASHINGTON, D.C., WAS DESIGNED BY JAMES HOBAN --WHO ALSO SUPERVISED ITS CONSTRUCTION-- *FOR A TOTAL FEE OF $500*

AN **EAR CAP** WAS ADVERTISED BY A SHOP IN LONDON, ENGLAND, IN THE 1800's, *TO REMEDY "PROMINENT EARS"*

EGGPLANT SHAPED LIKE A HUMAN HEAD *WITH EYES, NOSE AND A MOUTH* Submitted by MICHAEL L. MOORMAN, Mound City, Mo.

MACK WEAVER OF CROWELL, TEXAS, WHO WAS ELECTED COUNTY ATTORNEY IN 1893, *WAS REVEALED TO BE A SMALL SCRAWNY JACKASS*

STEPHEN GIRARD (1750–1831) A PHILADELPHIA, PA., BANKER, STARTED HIS CAREER AS A POOR CABIN BOY, BUT IN 1814 *HE OFFERED TO LOAN THE HARD-PRESSED U.S. GOVERNMENT $5,000,000*

THE **ELLIOTT HOUSE** ON THE DETROIT RIVER, NEAR AMHERSTBURG, ONTARIO, BUILT IN 1784, *IS ONTARIO'S OLDEST HOUSE*

THE MAN WHOSE FATE PURSUED HIM TO THE ENDS OF THE EARTH
CHARLES B. HENRY, A MEMBER OF THE GREELY ARCTIC EXPEDITION OF 1881
IN WHICH 15 MEN DIED OF HUNGER AND EXPOSURE WHILE THEIR
PARTY WAS STRANDED IN THE BITTER COLD FOR THREE YEARS
WAS EXECUTED BY HIS FELLOW EXPLORERS FOR STEALING FOOD—
IT WAS SUBSEQUENTLY DISCOVERED THAT THE CULPRIT'S TRUE NAME ACTUALLY
WAS CHARLES HENRY BUCK, A MURDERER WHO HAD JOINED THE AMERICAN
EXPEDITION AFTER HAVING ESCAPED FROM PRISON _WHILE AWAITING TRIAL_

NICHOLAS LONGWORTH
(1782-1863), OF CINCINNATI, OHIO,
ATTORNEY, HORTICULTURIST AND WINEGROWER,
LEFT AN ESTATE OF MORE THAN $15,000,000--
YET HE DRESSED SO *SHABBILY* THAT HE WAS
OFTEN MISTAKEN FOR A *TRAMP*

A **STEREOSCOPE**
USED FOR VIEWING
SLIDES IN THE
1860's— AN
ARABIC
INSCRIPTION
SET IN ITS LID
AND ENCRUSTED
WITH PRECIOUS
JEWELS

PIGEONS
COULD BE RAISED IN
FRANCE BEFORE THE
FRENCH REVOLUTION
ONLY BY NOBLEMEN

KING FREDERICK THE GREAT (1712-1786) OF PRUSSIA, WHO BECAME A GREAT MILITARY LEADER, AS A YOUTH HATED THE LIFE OF A SOLDIER SO BITTERLY THAT HE TRIED TO RUN AWAY-- AND HIS FATHER CONSIDERED EXECUTING HIM AS A DESERTER

"Jenny"
A 2-YEAR-OLD GERMAN SHEPHERD-SIBERIAN HUSKY OWNED BY JERRY K. GERBRACHT OF SAN FRANCISCO, CALIF., CLIMBS TREES TO A HEIGHT OF 40 FEET.

"Jenny" HAS BEEN GRANTED OFFICIAL PERMISSION TO SCALE TREES BY THE SAN FRANCISCO PARK DEPARTMENT

THE ELEPHANT FISH OF AFRICA, HAS A LONG TRUNKLIKE SNOUT

163

THE OLD TERRITORIAL PENITENTIARY
IN SANTA FE, NEW MEXICO,
WAS ERECTED IN THE CITY BECAUSE LOCAL OFFICIALS
GIVEN THE CHOICE OF A PRISON OR A STATE UNIVERSITY,
CHOSE THE PENITENTIARY

W. PIERCE
Died
Feb 31, 1860
Aged
73 years

TOMBSTONE
In Picton, Ont.,
CARRYING THE
DATE OF DEATH
AS FEB. 31
Submitted by
Jules Henry Marr
ALBUQUERQUE, N.M.

THE JUMPING MOUSE
USING ITS TAIL AS A BALANCER,
CAN LEAP 12 FEET

THE TUATARA
OF NEW ZEALAND,
LIVES AS LONG AS *300 YEARS*

THE **GIANT DOME** A 62-FOOT STALAGMITE IN CARLSBAD CAVERNS, N.M., *RESEMBLES THE LEANING TOWER OF PISA*

THE **ANCIENT ROMAN BATHS OF CARACALLA** OUTSIDE ROME, ITALY, EXTEND NEARLY A QUARTER MILE AND *ACCOMMODATED 25,000 BATHERS AT A TIME*

THE **WATERLOO WAR MEDAL** AWARDED TO ALL SOLDIERS WHO PARTICIPATED IN THAT DEFEAT OF NAPOLEON, DEPICTS VICTORY SEATED ON A PEDESTAL ... *A REPRODUCTION OF A COIN MINTED 2,265 YEARS EARLIER*

SOUTHWARK THEATER in Philadelphia, Pa.,
PROVIDED THE STAGE IN 1767 FOR THE
PREMIERE OF "THE PRINCE OF PARTHIA,"
*THE FIRST PROFESSIONAL PLAY
BY AN AMERICAN*

THE
VICEROY BUTTERFLY
WHICH IS PALATABLE
TO PREDATORS,
AVOIDS ENEMIES BY
EXACTLY DUPLICATING
THE APPEARANCE
OF THE MONARCH
BUTTERFLY, WHICH
IS UNPALATABLE

TOMBS, 25 FEET SQUARE,
ARE CONSTRUCTED FOR HONORED MEN OF THE
BETSILEO TRIBE OF MADAGASCAR, AND THE SKULLS AND
HORNS OF BULLOCKS SLAUGHTERED TO FEED THE
MOURNERS ADORN THE MEMORIAL

TEDDY ROOSEVELT (1858-1919) 26th PRESIDENT OF THE UNITED STATES, WAS SO NEARSIGHTED THAT IN THE SPANISH-AMERICAN WAR HE CARRIED *12 EXTRA PAIRS OF GLASSES IN HIS POCKETS AND HAT LINING*

DASHIELL HAMMETT (1894-1961) THE AMERICAN CRIME NOVELIST WHO ORIGINATED THE SCHOOL OF TOUGH THRILLERS, WROTE THE FIVE BOOKS THAT WON HIM FAME IN A PERIOD OF FOUR YEARS--AND *NEVER WROTE ANOTHER BOOK*

LIQUIDS
IN ANCIENT ROME, WERE OFTEN DISPENSED FROM VESSELS SHAPED *LIKE A SANDALED FOOT*

THE **OLDEST LIVING THING!** A RED CYPRESS STILL GROWING NEAR TAIPEI, TAIWAN, 173 FEET HIGH AND 88.44 FEET IN CIRCUMFERENCE, DISCOVERED BY PROF. CHOW HUI-YEN OF THE COLLEGE OF CHINESE CULTURE IN TAIWAN, IS MORE THAN 6,000 YEARS OLD

A **DAUGHTER**
IN THE COORG TRIBE OF INDIA, WHENEVER SHE MEETS HER FATHER, BOWS SO LOW *HER HANDS TOUCH THE GROUND*

A DYING MAN'S RIDDLE THAT REVEALED A FORTUNE!

ANDREW ASHLEY, A WEALTHY BUSINESSMAN, DYING IN HIS HOME IN LONDON, ENGLAND, IN 1908, WHISPERED AS HIS LAST WORDS: "*MONEY IN TILL.*" ASHLEY HAD OWNED 20 VOLUMES OF THE COLLECTED SERMONS OF THE REV. JOHN TILLOTSON -- WHICH HAD BEEN SENT AFTER HIS DEATH TO A BOOKDEALER -- *A FEW DAYS LATER THE BOOKSTORE RETURNED THE COLLECTION AS UNSALABLE* -- AND BETWEEN THE LOOSELY GLUED PAGES OF THE BOOKS WERE FOUND *140 ONE-THOUSAND-POUND NOTES* -- THE EQUIVALENT OF *$700,000!*

WILLIAM LINZEE PRESCOTT
OF DE LEON SPRINGS, FLA., IS A DIRECT DESCENDANT OF BOTH COL. WILLIAM PRESCOTT, WHO COMMANDED THE MINUTEMEN AT BUNKER HILL, AND OF CAPT. JOHN LINZEE, COMMANDER OF THE BRITISH SLOOP "FALCON," WHICH CANNONADED PRESCOTT'S TROOPS IN THAT BATTLE IN 1775

THE **MUMMIES** OF ANCIENT PERUVIANS WERE ENCASED IN FINE FABRICS AND GIVEN *A FALSE HEAD OF CLOTH* -- STUFFED WITH COTTON

A SUMMER WHITE HOUSE ON MT. FALCON NEAR DENVER, COLO., WAS TO BE BUILT WITH FUNDS RAISED BY PUBLIC SUBSCRIPTION IN 1911, AND A ROAD TO THE MOUNTAIN PEAK WAS COMPLETED, *BUT THE BUILDING NEVER PROGRESSED BEYOND THE CORNERSTONE AND ORNATE ARCHITECTURAL DRAWINGS*

NELLIE BLY
THE NEWSPAPER-
WOMAN WHO CIRCLED
THE WORLD IN 1889,
BEGAN HER CAREER
AT THE AGE OF 18
AFTER IMPRESSING
THE EDITOR OF THE
PITTSBURG DISPATCH
*BY A LETTER SHE
WROTE SUPPORTING
WOMEN'S RIGHTS*

"JUMBO"
THE FAMOUS P.T. BARNUM ELEPHANT OF THE 1880's THAT
WAS 10'7" HIGH AND WEIGHED 6 TONS, WOULD OBEY
NO ONE EXCEPT HIS TRAINER, MATTHEW SCOTT

171

ONLY 12 CONFEDERATE PENNIES WERE MINTED DURING THE ENTIRE CIVIL WAR

LUIGI PIRANDELLO (1867-1936) ITALIAN WINNER OF A NOBEL PRIZE FOR LITERATURE, DID NOT WRITE HIS FIRST PLAY UNTIL HE WAS 45 YEARS OF AGE

THE MOORE HOUSE in Yorktown, Va., IS THE HOME IN WHICH AMERICAN AND BRITISH OFFICERS MET TO DRAFT ENGLAND'S SURRENDER AFTER THE BATTLE OF YORKTOWN (Oct. 19, 1781)

THE COFFIN USED BY INNUIT ESKIMOS OF ALASKA WAS A PLANK BOX ELEVATED ABOVE THE GROUND, AND THE BODY WAS PLACED IN IT DOUBLED UP AND ON ITS SIDE

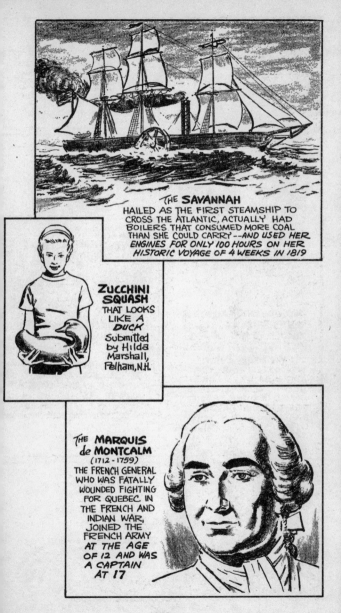

THE **SAVANNAH**
HAILED AS THE FIRST STEAMSHIP TO
CROSS THE ATLANTIC, ACTUALLY HAD
BOILERS THAT CONSUMED MORE COAL
THAN SHE COULD CARRY--AND *USED HER
ENGINES FOR ONLY 100 HOURS ON HER
HISTORIC VOYAGE OF 4 WEEKS IN 1819*

**ZUCCHINI
SQUASH**
THAT LOOKS
LIKE A
DUCK
Submitted
by Hilda
Marshall,
Pelham, N.H.

THE **MARQUIS
de MONTCALM**
(1712 - 1759)
THE FRENCH GENERAL
WHO WAS FATALLY
WOUNDED FIGHTING
FOR QUEBEC IN
THE FRENCH AND
INDIAN WAR,
JOINED THE
FRENCH ARMY
*AT THE AGE
OF 12 AND WAS
A CAPTAIN
AT 17*

173

The **LARVA** OF THE SPICE-BUSH SWALLOWTAIL BEFORE IT BECOMES A BUTTERFLY FRIGHTENS OFF PREDATORS BY WHAT APPEARS TO BE GLARING EYES AND A LARGE MOUTH-- *BUT BOTH ARE MERELY PIGMENTED CAMOUFLAGE*

The **WOMAN WHO CAUSED A U.S. PRESIDENT TO BE ORDERED OUT OF HIS VICE-PRESIDENT'S HOME !**

Mrs. Peggy Eaton, WIFE OF SECRETARY OF WAR JOHN H. EATON OF TENNESSEE, HAD SO SCANDALIZED THE WIVES OF OTHER CABINET MEMBERS THAT WHEN PRESIDENT ANDREW JACKSON CALLED ON MRS. JOHN C. CALHOUN, WIFE OF HIS VICE-PRESIDENT, TO ASK HER TO RECEIVE PEGGY SOCIALLY, *MRS. CALHOUN ASKED THE PRESIDENT TO LEAVE HER HOUSE*

The **ESCONDIDO BRANCH** OF THE UNIVERSITY OF SOUTHERN CALIFORNIA, CONSTRUCTED IN 1887, *WAS NEVER OPENED TO COLLEGE STUDENTS.* U.S.C. HAD ONLY 25 STUDENTS IN 1893, AND THE ESCONDIDO BUILDING BECAME A GRAMMAR AND HIGH SCHOOL

The **BOWHEAD WHALE** HAS A MOUTH ONE-THIRD AS LARGE AS ITS ENTIRE BODY

OLD NORTH CHURCH
IN BOSTON, MASS.,
IN WHICH THE SIGNAL
LANTERNS FOR PAUL REVERE
WERE POSTED IN APRIL,
1775, HAD DISCHARGED ITS
PASTOR AS A BRITISH
TORY JUST BEFORE THE
LANTERNS WERE PLACED
IN ITS STEEPLE

SIRIMAVO RATWATTE BADARANAIKE
of Ceylon,
IN 1960 BECAME THE WORLD'S
FIRST WOMAN PRIME MINISTER

THE BURIED CITY OF TUHUOLO
TAKLA MAKAN DESERT, CHINA,
THE ENTIRE CITY OF TUHUOLO HAS BEEN ALMOST
COMPLETELY COVERED BY SHIFTING SANDS FOR **2,000** YEARS

STEPHEN COLLINS FOSTER
(1826-1864) WHO WROTE SONGS THAT EXTOLLED
FAMILY AND HOME, DIED HOMELESS IN A
HOSPITAL CHARITY WARD

JOSEPH A. WHITE
of Deerfield Beach, Fla.,
PARTICIPATING IN THE
PEOPLE'S DAY REGATTA
IN PHILADELPHIA, PA.,
ROWED IN 6 RACES IN
ONE DAY AND RAN
2 MILES TO MAKE
THE REQUIRED 145-
POUND WEIGHT FOR
ONE OF THE EVENTS
July 5, 1926

THE **CATTLEYA ORCHID**
PRODUCES 5,000,000
SEEDS IN A SINGLE
SEED CASE.
IF EVEN 10 PERCENT
OF THE ORCHID SEEDS
REACHED MATURITY,
THE EARTH'S SURFACE
WOULD BE CARPETED
WITH ORCHIDS

THE MOST ASTOUNDING DIVING FEAT IN ALL HISTORY! STOTTI GEORGHIOS, A GREEK SPONGE FISHERMAN, WITH NO GOGGLES, FINS OR BREATHING EQUIPMENT OF ANY KIND, DESCENDED **200** FEET IN THE ADRIATIC SEA IN 1913 TO RECOVER AN ANCHOR LOST FROM AN ITALIAN BATTLESHIP--*AND REMAINED DOWN FOR 4 MINUTES!* THE PRESSURE ON HIS BODY WAS 103 POUNDS PER SQUARE INCH --YET HE SUFFERED NO ILL EFFECTS

THE "JEANNETTE"
ON AN ARCTIC EXPLORATION, WAS CRUSHED AND
SANK IN 1881 AFTER HAVING BEEN FROZEN
FAST FOR NEARLY 2 YEARS

THE CAPITOL IN WILLIAMSBURG, VA.,
FROM ITS OPENING IN 1704, UNTIL 1723
BARRED FIRE, CANDLES AND SMOKING

THE OLDEST WRITTEN
POLITICAL HISTORY
A CLAY POT
BEARING IN THE SUMERIAN LANGUAGE
THE STORY OF THE CITY OF
UMMA'S ATTEMPT AT CONQUEST
-- COMPILED BY A KING OF LAGASH
IN ANCIENT BABYLONIA SOME
4,500 YEARS AGO

A **MONUMENT** IN MAR MUNENE, KASAI, IN THE CONGO, COMMEMORATES THE FIRST DIAMOND FOUND IN THE AREA

GEORGE MORRISON A YOUNG AUSTRALIAN DOCTOR, WALKED ALONE ACROSS CHINA IN 1895 FROM SHANGHAI TO RANGOON, ALTHOUGH HE COULD NOT SPEAK CHINESE --TO MAKE HIMSELF INCONSPICUOUS HE HAD A PIGTAIL PINNED IN HIS HAT

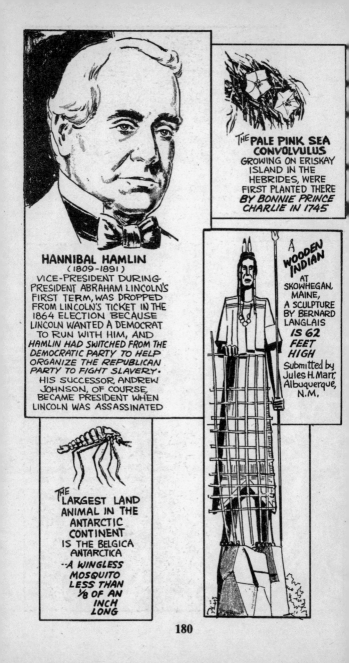

HANNIBAL HAMLIN
(1809-1891)
VICE-PRESIDENT DURING PRESIDENT ABRAHAM LINCOLN'S FIRST TERM, WAS DROPPED FROM LINCOLN'S TICKET IN THE 1864 ELECTION BECAUSE LINCOLN WANTED A DEMOCRAT TO RUN WITH HIM, AND HAMLIN HAD SWITCHED FROM THE DEMOCRATIC PARTY TO HELP ORGANIZE THE REPUBLICAN PARTY TO FIGHT SLAVERY.
HIS SUCCESSOR, ANDREW JOHNSON, OF COURSE, BECAME PRESIDENT WHEN LINCOLN WAS ASSASSINATED

THE **PALE PINK SEA CONVOLVULUS** GROWING ON ERISKAY ISLAND IN THE HEBRIDES, WERE FIRST PLANTED THERE *BY BONNIE PRINCE CHARLIE IN 1745*

A **WOODEN INDIAN** AT SKOWHEGAN, MAINE, A SCULPTURE BY BERNARD LANGLAIS *IS 62 FEET HIGH*
Submitted by Jules H. Marr, Albuquerque, N.M.

THE **LARGEST LAND ANIMAL IN THE ANTARCTIC CONTINENT** IS THE BELGICA ANTARCTICA -- *A WINGLESS MOSQUITO LESS THAN* $1/8$ *OF AN INCH LONG*

180

THE LARGEST MONOLITH IN THE WORLD
AYERS ROCK NEAR ALICE SPRINGS, AUSTRALIA,
A GREAT STONE COLUMN 1,100 FEET HIGH,
HAS A BIGGER AREA THAN THE CITY OF LONDON

THE **TURKEY FEATHER DUSTER** WAS INVENTED BY WILLIAM HOAG OF CHICAGO, ILL., IN 1872, WHILE HE WAS SNOW-BOUND IN MONTICELLO, IOWA

7 TOMATOES THAT GREW IN ONE CLUSTER
Submitted by Frank H. Christopher, Jr., Colonial Beach, Va.

ONE TIME CONGRESS VOTED RIGHT!
CAPT. JOHN CLEVES SYMMES, A HERO OF THE WAR OF 1812, ASKED CONGRESS TO FINANCE AN EXPEDITION TO THE EARTH'S INTERIOR BY DRILLING HOLES AT THE NORTH AND SOUTH POLES.. *CONGRESS TURNED HIM DOWN-- BUT HE GOT 25 AFFIRMATIVE VOTES*

HERNANDO CORTEZ
AND HIS SPANISH FOLLOWERS, WHO CONQUERED
MEXICO, CONSIDERED THE JADE PIECES THEY
OBTAINED FROM THE INDIANS A CURE FOR
KIDNEY AILMENTS --CALLING THEM **"PIEDRAS
DE YJADA"** OR **"STONES OF THE SIDE,"**
FROM YJADA COMES OUR WORD JADE

HALLOCK CASTLE IN New Haven, Conn.,
WAS BUILT BY GERALD HALLOCK AS A REPLICA
OF ENGLAND'S KENILWORTH CASTLE

THE SHREW
THE SMALLEST FUR-BEARING
ANIMAL IN NORTH AMERICA,
*EATS MORE THAN 3 TIMES
ITS OWN WEIGHT EVERY DAY*

The **WRITING HORSE** Germinal A HORSE OWNED BY A FRENCHMAN NAMED ROUHET WAS TRAINED TO WRITE ITS OWNER'S NAME *WITH A BRUSH HELD IN ITS MOUTH*

The **BRIDE** in Malaya, IS CONCEALED DURING THE WEDDING CEREMONY --REMAINING BEHIND A WHITE CURTAIN WHICH SURROUNDS AN ORNATE BEDSTEAD THAT IS KEPT IN HER HOUSE FOR TWO MONTHS.

THE BEARS THAT MAKE HOUSE CALLS

TAME BEARS IN ROMANIA, ARE TRAINED BY THEIR GYPSY OWNERS TO TREAT PEOPLE WITH BACKACHES *BY GIVING MASSAGES*

A HUNTER

IN THE MURIA TRIBE, INDIA, ALWAYS STARTS HIS HUNT BY *BOWING IN WORSHIP TO HIS AXE, BOW AND ARROWS*

A HORSE OF A DIFFERENT COLOR

WILLIAM COOMBS A MILLER
of Blatchington, England,
PAINTED HIS HORSE A DIFFERENT COLOR
EACH WEEK FOR 22 YEARS

THE ANIMAL WAS ALTERNATELY
YELLOW, GREEN, BLUE AND PURPLE

ST. ANDREW'S CROSS HAS BEEN FLOWN BY THE SCOTTISH PEOPLE FOR HUNDREDS OF YEARS-- YET IT HAS NEVER BEEN OFFICIALLY ADOPTED AS THE FLAG OF *SCOTLAND*

GERALD "DOC" DOHERTY OF THE UNIV. OF DELAWARE, IN ONE FOOTBALL GAME CARRIED THE BALL ONLY 6 TIMES AND *RAN IT 220 YARDS* -OCT. 21, 1946-

THE **WINDSOR HOTEL** IN DENVER, COLORADO, OPENED IN 1880 WITH *A TAPROOM STUDDED WITH 3,000 SILVER DOLLARS*

186

SOD HOMES BUILT BY SETTLERS IN NEBRASKA, IN THE 1800's, ARE STILL USABLE AFTER 100 YEARS -- *YET, THEIR TOTAL CON-STRUCTION COST OFTEN WAS ONLY $5*

A **LOCOMOTIVE** OF THE BRIDGTON AND HARRISON R.R., IN MAINE, JUMPED THE TRACK IN 1930 *ON THE DAY THE ROAD BEGAN OPERATIONS..* THE RAILROAD CEASED OPERATIONS THE SAME YEAR

A **STATUE** IN THE EXACT LIKENESS OF THE CORPSE WAS ENTOMBED WITH THE MUMMY IN ANCIENT EGYPT IN THE BELIEF THAT THIS "DUPLICATE BODY" COULD *ENJOY ALL THE OFFERINGS OF THE FUNERAL*

JULIA CLIFFORD LATHROP (1858-1932) FIRST CHIEF OF THE CHILDREN'S BUREAU OF THE UNITED STATES DEPARTMENT OF LABOR, WAS *THE FIRST WOMAN TO HEAD A U.S. GOV'T. BUREAU*

The CATHEDRAL BELL THAT CAME FROM WAR AND RETURNED TO WAR!
THE CATHEDRAL OF COLOGNE, Germany, WAS FITTED IN 1874 WITH A 25-TON BELL MADE FROM FRENCH GUNS CAPTURED IN THE WAR OF 1870 -- AND IN WORLD WAR I *THE GERMANS MELTED DOWN THE BELL TO MAKE WEAPONS FOR USE AGAINST THE FRENCH*

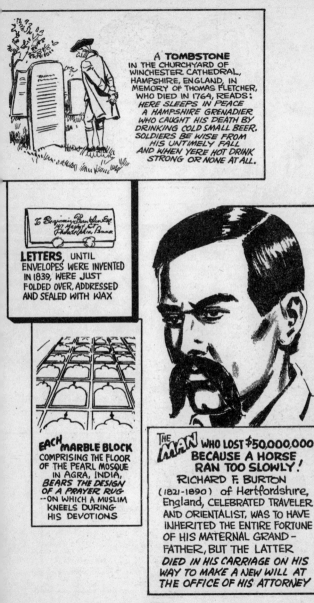

A **TOMBSTONE** IN THE CHURCHYARD OF WINCHESTER CATHEDRAL, HAMPSHIRE, ENGLAND, IN MEMORY OF THOMAS FLETCHER, WHO DIED IN 1764, READS:
HERE SLEEPS IN PEACE A HAMPSHIRE GRENADIER WHO CAUGHT HIS DEATH BY DRINKING COLD SMALL BEER. SOLDIERS BE WISE FROM HIS UNTIMELY FALL AND WHEN YERE HOT DRINK STRONG OR NONE AT ALL.

LETTERS, UNTIL ENVELOPES WERE INVENTED IN 1839, WERE JUST FOLDED OVER, ADDRESSED AND SEALED WITH WAX

EACH MARBLE BLOCK COMPRISING THE FLOOR OF THE PEARL MOSQUE IN AGRA, INDIA, *BEARS THE DESIGN OF A PRAYER RUG* --ON WHICH A MUSLIM KNEELS DURING HIS DEVOTIONS

THE **MAN** WHO LOST $50,000,000 **BECAUSE A HORSE RAN TOO SLOWLY!** RICHARD F. BURTON (1821-1890) of Hertfordshire, England, CELEBRATED TRAVELER AND ORIENTALIST, WAS TO HAVE INHERITED THE ENTIRE FORTUNE OF HIS MATERNAL GRAND-FATHER, BUT THE LATTER *DIED IN HIS CARRIAGE ON HIS WAY TO MAKE A NEW WILL AT THE OFFICE OF HIS ATTORNEY*

THOMAS CARLYLE
(1795 - 1881)
THE FAMOUS SCOTTISH AUTHOR ONCE LABORED **5 MONTHS** ON THE FIRST VOLUME OF HIS MONUMENTAL HISTORY OF THE FRENCH REVOLUTION -- *ONLY TO HAVE A FRIEND'S CARELESS SERVANT USE IT TO START A FIRE*

OGARITA BOOTH
THE ACTRESS DAUGHTER OF JOHN WILKES BOOTH, PRESIDENT LINCOLN'S ASSASSIN, ALWAYS WORE A MEDALLION CONTAINING A *PHOTO OF BOOTH*

THE **LLOYD NECK OAK**
IN HUNTINGTON, LONG ISLAND, N.Y., A RED OAK THAT IN 450 YEARS GREW TO A HEIGHT OF 90 FT., WITH A TRUNK 20 FT. IN CIRCUMFERENCE *AND A LIMB SPREAD OF 140 FEET*

NICKEL COIN
A 9-YEAR-OLD MARE TRAINED ON A DIET OF
DUCK EGGS AND BEER, WON ENGLAND'S
FAMED GRAND NATIONAL STEEPLECHASE IN
1951 IN A RACE IN WHICH ONLY 3 OF
THE 36 STARTERS FINISHED

THE SUMMER PALACE
OF THE EMPRESS DOWAGER OF CHINA,
BUILT SIX MILES NORTHWEST OF PEKING IN THE
19TH CENTURY, INCLUDES A HUGE MARBLE
BUILDING SHAPED LIKE A BOAT

CHANDELIER
WITH 5 BULBS WHICH
WERE INSTALLED IN 1925,
AND ARE STILL
**BURNING
50 YEARS
LATER**
In the home of
Harry E. Blank,
Covington, Ky.

THE TOWN HALL
OF VENDÔME, FRANCE,
WAS LOCATED ABOVE THE TOWN
GATE FOR **473 YEARS**

A **RAKE** MADE BY
AMERICAN INDIANS
*FROM ANTLERS
OF A DEER*

THE TOOTHY BUDDHA
THE BUDDHA OF TATUNG, CHINA, IS THE ONLY BUDDHA
STATUE ... *THAT SHOWS ITS TEETH*

192